CONDITION OF PEASANTS IN INDIA (200 - 600 AD)

CONDITION OF PEASANTS IN INDIA (200 - 600 AD)

Lalita Kumari

Translator:- **Birendra Kumar**

KALPAZ

ISBN: 978-93-5128-045-3

Price: ₹ 450

First Edition, 2014

Published by

Kalpaz Publications
C-30, Satyawati Nagar,
Delhi – 110052
E-mail: kalpaz@hotmail.com
Ph.: 9212142040

Laser Typesetting: Gyan Print (AB-I)
Printed at: G. Print Process, Delhi

Cataloging in Publication Data—DK
Courtesy: D.K. Agencies (P) Ltd. <docinfo@dkagencies.com>

Lalita Kumari.
Condition of peasants in India (200-600 AD) / Lalita Kumari.
p. cm.
Includes bibliographical references (p.).
ISBN 9789351280453

1. Peasants—India—History—To 1500. 2. Agriculture—India—History—To 1500. I. Title.

DDC 305.56330954 23

Contents

Introduction

History is the chronological study of the past or past events. Usually a chronological record of events, as of the life or development of a people or institution, often includes an explanation of those events. The past records of events always contain activities of the rulers and their state (kingdom). But as of now there have been fundamental changes in this concept of history and no more it is a complition of more royal activities. Now, history is being linked to activities of common masses by dint of whose labour society and state has come up bit by bit. These common men mainly include peasants — a producing class, who hold the key in laying the foundation of the country's economy. These peasants have been the principal factors of civilisation and production whose valuable contributions play a significant role in economic development of every country. Therefore, in order to assess the real foundation, economic life and development of any country's culture, it is essential to know about the peasants.

In this book, the economic life of peasants in different periods has been discussed. But it has always lacked in exhaustive details. The period between 200 AD to 600 AD has been a transitional phase in Indian history. During these times, the study about the chief producing class peasants was not found adequate. The past records show that the roles of the peasants which are the largest part of the population always play an important role in the process of development. While illustrating the historical qualities of peasants, Chayanor and Mao tse Tung explained in two different lines in as much as they had been expressed contradictory views. Yet, both of them clearly described about the peasants as a class whose lives changes in the backdrop of their resistance and potential.

The European historians wrote Indian history with a touch of negative vibes as they termed the Indians were not well-aware of history at all. On its own, this attitude preseumed to be a myth and this was propagated vigorously by imperialist historians while the truth stands otherwise. From very early times awareness of history is found amongst (Indians) history as a subject that provided education of economics, religion pleasure and salvation i.e., (*Artha, Kama, Dharma and Moksha*). Possibly this may be incomplete and to a great extent, narrow definition of history. But if we consider this in the context of time this was far too much a reason of thinking attented in advance.

In order to study peasants, it is necessary to study economic history of that age. Study of ancient economic history began when lesson in the middle of 19th century in his book (Indishi Altarre Tooms Kunde[1] ??) threw sufficient light on Industry and Commerce. Following this so many books were written which were related to Economic history. Richard Fick[2] in his book on Economic history based on Buddhist sources described commerce and classes. Riz Davids[3] in his work Buddhist India threw light on North Indian economic systems. But all these scholars tried mainly to describe the caste system of India. They just threw a passing glance on economic life. Besides these N.C. Bandyopadhyay[4] in his work Economic life and progress in Ancient India has described economic system of early period. There is an important book on economic organisation by C.H. Robinson,[5]— the Intercourse between India and the Western world. In this book, Robinson described commercial relations between India and Greece, Roman Empire since the ancient times till the downfall of Rome. But in all of such books this fact was asserted that Indian society since its birth had remained unchanged.[6]

Such thoughts of English historians were challenged by Indian historians, who came under the influence of national movement and started writing under its influence and very clearly opposed the imperialist line. At the end of 19th century development of nationalism and political consciousness, Indian scholars made the people aware of economic exploitation of India by Britishers.

M.A. Booch,[7] N.C. Bandyohaohyay,[8] M.K., Das[9] and Prananath[10] in the third decade of 20th century produced exhaustive details of ancient Indian commerce and economic institution on the basis of literary texts. Booch in his book discussed property rights, currency system and prices, commerce and communication, public finance, etc. But he did not touch on developments of special qualities of ancient Indian Economic. So far as agriculture, animal husbandry related rural economy is concerned, describing land organisation, agriculture, industry and commerce was specially highlighted by Bandyopadhyay as well attempted to properly study economic development. He claims to have done period-wise division keeping in mind economic powers and special events.[11] In fact, Indian nationalist historians in order to oppose Britishers ignored many realities in order to underline glorious past. Samaddar, who was supportive of British Empire and Prananath, who emphasised economic activities barring such exception almost all contemporary historians were inspired by nationalist view point. They were inspired by the nationalist influence consciously or unconsciously, they always tried to show that their economic condition in the past was better than their present condition. As a result, the study of ancient economic history spread so many illusions. Naming Gupta period, economically as golden period was one such flight of imagination.

There are several other works on this subject amongst them. The Hindu Revenue System by U.N. Ghosal[12] was the 1st thoughtful study of its kind. Opposing V.M. Smith on some issues, he has written that very few clear proofs are available to prove that in the ancient and medieval periods taxation was so high that barely anything was left for the livelihood of the peasant. U.N. Ghosal has supported his views also in his second book — The Agrarian System in Ancient India.[13] He has written one complete chapter on the ownership of land and has enunciated that in Brahminical laws there is no clear glance of nominal ownership of land, rather of chief specialities and virtues of personal ownership finds clear mention.

But during 5th and 6th decades of 20th century main trends observed in the ancient Indian economic history was represented by such writers, who under the influences of socialist ideology and materialist description of history have drawn their conclusions. A.N. Bose leads such historians who have produced study of North Indian rural economic between 600 BC.— 2004[14] A.D. Names of B.N. Dutta[15] and S.A. Dange need special mention. D.D. Kosambi[16] has tried to understand exhaustive study of ancient economic history from Marxist angle. According to him to produce means of production and its graduals changes chronologically is history. Though a Marxiest Kosambi does not produced any concrete evidence of forms of slavery, system, feudalism, capitalism in rigid forms. Origin of slavery system, expansion and its nature has been described in details by another Marxist historian Devraj Chanana in his work, "Slavery in Ancient India".[17] Ram Saran Sharma through some of his works and essays has tried to scientifically analyse ancient Indian economic history, which is satisfactory to a great extent.[18] D.N. Jha through his book Revenue System in Post Mauryan and Gupta Times has described and analysed economic history of this mentioned period substantively.[19]

S. K. Maity is the only historian, who has written one book exclusively on economic history of Gupta period.[20] The book Economic Life of Northern India was published in 1957. Wherein Economic life during Gupta period has exclusively been described. Aspects of ancient Indian Economic History within a short period of time was also studied by M.H. Gopal. In this book, Mauryan Public Finance through light on Mauryan Economic as described in Arthasastra on the basis of new facts.[21] This book also includes economic history since the downfalls of Mauryans and entire Gupta period. Where the possibility of feudalisation of land-holding system has been denied by Maity, Gopal have tried to draw the conclusions of the nationalist historiography.

So far as rural economy of India during Gupta period is concerned, these writers have drawn out their conclusions without combining the changes occurring on the course of time in their writings, due to which they lack scientific and substantive study. Cambridge History of Indian in several volumes is a detailed study of Indian history of various periods. In the first volume of the same good enough detail of Indian social and economic history is provided. But economic history does not study economic developments and holistic pictures of different phases do not emerge out of this.

Initially, two-three centuries prior to Gupta period is known as Dark age, it is believed that both culture and civilisation had a decline in this age, but in economic history it does not look dark at all. The historians essentially towards it draw attention in the economic developments of this period. First among the works during this period is "Life in Gupta Period" by R.N. Soletor. This work depicts the life between

300 to 750 A.D. In this work, the writer has tried to through light on all aspects of life, but the description of economic life can not be termed satisfactiory. It mainly act in accordance with the facts provided by Barak Miler and Amar Singh. Another work is edited by R.C. Mazumdar and A.S. Altekar in 6th volume of Indian people as this includes the description of both political history and economic life of the people of that period.[22] Third work Classical Age is edited by R.C. Mazumdar and A.D. Pusalkar in which many writers presented detailed study of Indian history between 320 to 740 A.D.[23] Though economic life during Gupta and post-Gupta period has been covered by U.N. Ghosal, but it lacks in clarity and throught that has emerged due to recent researches.

On ancient India and its economic history alone several books and research articles have been published in scholastic magazines but compared with their on Indian agriculture and conditions of peasants between 200 to 600 A.D., there is total scarcity of well-arranged and orderly study on this matter. Since the ancient period, agriculture and the principal contributors of the farmers were the backbone of Indian economy, therefore, on this subject (200 to 600 A.D.), an in-depth study is utmost important to know the actual picture.

It has been seen that the four-hundred years of post-Maurya and Gupta period between 200 AD to 600 AD of the Indian society and economy underwent important and ciritcal changes. During this period, the process of partial feudalisation of land holding holding system began.[24] So much light has been thrown on characteristics and other aspects of feudalism in Indian historiography. In this connection, an important story comes to light from the correspondence between Angles and Marx. Addressing Marx, Angles wrote from London on 22nd December 1882 in which he had mentioned that serfdom and bonded labour may not be the manifestation of middle age feudal-social structure alone. Keeping the time and space of individual in mind, if we see them in the context of the all historical events where the landlords forced to work people from the lower strata in the interest of their pleasure and amenities, who toiled hard in agriculture and agricultural-related works which eventually gave birth to feudal society in that era. Paul M. Sweezy while considering the definition of Maurice Daub has offered this as a vital point during debate. It seems that according to the views of the Historians, the lives of poor people and labourer classes were pathetic as they were exploited by the upper classes in a merciless way due to their helplessness. In this context, the discussion of transition from feudalism to capitalism is very important. Feudalism held its overwhelming grip in the society where the common men were the subject of their feudal tendencies in inhuman way. The over-exploitation and feudal nature of the upper class took a new shape in the form exploitation-machinery in India during Gupta period.

A new aspect and dimension of feudalism is also traced in the booklet of Robert S. Hoyet Feudal institution, causes and consequences of decentralisation. He writes in the introduction of above noted booklets that the word 'feudalism' has been used in a very wrong and illusive way. Even in practical life at a psychological level, this word is practiced. For example – in newspaper and magazines or books the writers or editors, if they refuse to accept any view or fact on this point he is understood to be feudal. In this context, one who is by his nature is noble or licentious or reactionary can also be called feudal, because of his holding a higher position and status maintains a pro-power or bureaucratic control over his subordinate officers is also conveyed the same meaning. Flouting equality on democratic states or going against these terms, and unnatural action taken is also considered to be feudalism. Thus, 'feudal' word became synonymous to 'mean' and 'low'. Other words it also encouraged hatred and cursed-caste system of feudalism in Gupta period on the touch-stone of above mentioned context. It looks only as a cancer because caste system from the past, as a social deformity became most poisonous on account of unsavoury feudal conduct. So, the cursed-caste system coupled with feudalism provided Indian society a peculiar form.

At the initial phases of this feudalism in the northern and eastern parts of Bengal and Madhya Pradesh, cultivable land was allotted to the priest of the temple and the Brahmins depicted enough to evidences to corroborate this fact. Elaborate tradition of grant land in the villages became a speciality of rule of Gupta period. Central rulers relaxed their grip on the sources of revenues of the gifted lands in the villages. Various sources of revenues were left on the will of the beneficiaries. Gradually, as the Brahmin class started enjoying gift and landowner rights connected to the ruling class grew in numbers. The beneficiaries left the attitude of hereditary livelihood in the same manners. As a result, the Brahmins left their traditional occupation of *Purohit* and in place of it they were established their link with land and involved in direct administrative arrangement of villages donated to them in the gifts. This class of beneficiaries, benefitted due to donations, emerged as feudal class which got the term of parasitical in the social strata. They erected several walls of barriers and were destroyed the rural economic arrangements by exploiting the lower class to their hilt during Gupta period.

Highly developed and well-established economic system of Maurya period was shattered in the name of caste, creed, religion and untouchability and thus this feudal class enormously damaged the social fabric of the Indian society. As a result of total domination of this tradition in the villages vitiate the agriculture and rural atmosphere to make it more and more poisonous. In Gangetic areas, Gujarat and Maharashtra villages earlier established, spreaded this tradition which were denoted. On the basis of literary and archaeological sources and study of economic system through enough evidences on the process of development of feudalism.

Due to donation of land and the instances of fragmentation of land in this age has also been observed. These unethical processes prove to be highly injurious for the cause of agricultural operations. It could be seen as a well-conceived conspiracy so that peasants and land owners could not get united. Brahmins and other beneficiaries were getting benefits of several tax and administrative amenities. As a result, a new class of land owners cropped up. Measurement of land, sale and purchase, shape and size of agricultural land, made a negative impact on the peasants and land owners to make their lives miserable. With the advent of feudalism due to land organisation system a big gap emerged to aggravate their problems. Consequently, this change had no creative impact on village (rural) economy. Feudalisation took the centerstage and its negative impact made a big blow gradually in religious and social life of the people.

In order to get a true picture of process first we will have to lean towards archaeological sources. To know the history of Gupta dynasty, their then emperiors left many inscriptions which were very much helpful and also could have been found from various places in northern part of India. Leaving aside some exceptions, we are certain about the origin and time of almost all these points. Out of these inscriptions, Kumar Gupta's inscription on copper plate from Damodarpur (443-448 AD), Dhanaidah copper plate inscription (443 AD), copper plate inscription of Indore (465 AD) and inscription of Garhawa are very important. Besides these Malie copper plate inscription of (571-72 AD) of Dharsen IInd Sanchi Stone inscription of Chandra Gupta II also provide us important informations.

Besides these, governmental inscriptions of Gupta period also deserve equal importance. For example there are certain Royal Edicts amongst governmental inscriptions, but generally they are administrative charters (letter) or land gift letters. Royal Edicts contain multi-dimensional achievement; victories of the kings and religious gifts donated by them, such things have been chanted. In this category, falls the inscription of Allahabad of Samudragupta. From these inscriptions, we know about kings of different categories and their relations with Samudragupta whom he had won and who were treated as subordinate feudal lords and officers.

Prayag Royal inscription of Samudra Gupta describes and talks about feudalism wherein he descusses about returning the kingdoms of higher class again and while doing this states let them live independent but they pay taxes to me, obey me, put our signs on their flags and be present in my court and pay respect to me. Several types of taxes have been mentioned there in i.e., Uparikar, Udrang, Visti, Hiranya etc. On the third side we know about one new genre of donations i.e., land grant. Now, the number of such grants started to grow in numbers in which kings and land-owners becoming pleased by some works of any person in order to carry out works of any *Math*, Temple or educational institutions donated land, village or an area were given to him. Here in, donor, donee, gifted land, related officers, realised taxes cause of gift, purchase writers name, name of the witness, condition of donation, the longevity of donations, etc., have been mentioned.

Inscriptions of land donations of this period have been found out from western India. During *Vakatak* empires we know something about mainly central India, western Deccan and some parts of Gujarat, and other side of Vindhyas, Parivrajak Maharaj had ruled central part. We get to know a lot about economic system of Gupta Period.[25] As a source of economic history, inscriptions-related to land gifts hold special place. There in, them, expansion of agriculture, self-dependent economic system land ownership, rate of productivity, relation between agriculture and different cottage industries, fragmentation of farming area on various aspects of these enough light has been thrown.

In order to know the economic history of this period literary source also will have to be taken into account. Amongst religious sources, law books holds unique place. Smriti books in true form were written in Gupta period. Famous law books of this period are *Vishnu Smriti, Narad Smriti, Yagyavalkya Smriti, and Katyayan Smriti* etc.

With the beginning of Christian era, *Dharmashastras* were replaced by *Smritis.* It was written between 200 BC and 9th century AD. But most of the *Smitris* were written in prose form and composed in the form of poetry. Subjects discussed in *Dharmashastras* have been discussed in *Smitris* in much greater details; along with those new subjects also have been included. *Manusmitri* is considered to be the oldest among *Smitris.* German scholar Buhler considers it to have been composed between 200 BC – to 200 AD. There are such chapters in it which can be comfortably placed in 5th century AD. In its 10th chapter, there is description of 61 hybrids caste, who came often by exogamous process i.e., if a *Brahmin* lady with a *Sudra* produces a child, the child will be called *Chandal* and such birth is known as exogamous. Many such exogamous castes are described in *Manusmriti,* most of them have been placed in the category of *Sudras* and *Antyaj.* According to Manusmriti, Shudras and woman have been graded low and were looked down upon. On the other hand, Brahmins have been assigned very special status and they were provided with many privileges.

Whatever it may be for creed, caste and family institutions, history, there is enough material in Manusmriti. *Smritis* by

Yagyavalkya, Narad, Brishaspati and Katyayan are considered most prominent *Smritis* of Gupta period. During post-Gupta period, Parasar *Smriti* also contains enough useful materials. In all these Smritis particularly in Narad *Smriti,* maximum privileges were bestowed upon *Brahmin varna.* In *Smritis,* there is long description of Daibhag, a commentary on Manusmriti what was the place of different types of sons in the family we know from this. In *Smritis,* we find *Vyawahar Khand, Achar Khand* and *Prayaschit Kand.* In *Vyawahar Khand,* rules have been framed for the improvement of group. These inform us how traders together combined to form guild and corporation and according to their investment share, profit was distributed. *Khandas* (volumes) containing *Achar* and *Prayaschit* throw light on social relations between different castes and their religious works. There is description of cleanliness and uncleanliness in *Achar.*

It has been discussed how a member of upper caste becomes impure through food and body contact. What to eat and what not to eat has also been discussed.

A study of *Prayaschit Khand* provides an idea that to get social rules implemented was not the responsibility of king alone because of the influence of *Brahministic* ideology there were provisions of several types of *Prayaschits.* Those who transgressed *Varna* and *Dharma,* consecration ceremonies they had to undergo *Prayaschits.* Clearly, because of social bindings only they had to do so, there was no involvement of king in this.

In between 7th century to 19th century, so many commentaries, interpretations and essays were written on the *Dharm Sutras* and *Smritis.* These writers explained these ancient laws particularly on Daibhage, several commentaries were written, because along with this there always raised the question of division of property. In all the commentaries, particular attention has been given on explaining Daibhage. There are seven commentaries available on Manusmriti. Amongst them, the commentaries written in 9th century by Medhatith is most famous. It helps us to understand the ancient laws in a better way. But at some places where commentators have interpreted ancient laws in the context of their own time, if we rely only on them, we do not get very clear idea about the intent of ancient *Dharmashastra* writers.

This is also worth mentioning that in *Dharmashastras* and commentaries on them same fact has been repeated time and again which makes people think that in ancient time Indian institutions totally lacked in any changes. But on same subject writers of *Dharmashastra* and their commentators have differed on their opinions. These opinions can be well-understood only in the context of space, time and prevailing situation correctly and this also indicates that social institutions were going under changes. For example according to *Dharma Sutras,* initially the numbers of cross-breed caste (hybrid caste) were only a dozen but in *Manusmritis* days it grows to sixty one.

Yagyavalkya *Smriti* is believed to have been written between 2nd and 4th century AD. In these materials of Manusmriti has been written in short and arranged in proper order. Yagyavalkya S*mriti* and a commentary-on *Mitakshara* written by Vigyaneshuwar of western India in 11th century and both taken together to provide basic material for Hindu civil law. A work like *Brihaspati smriti* in ancient India is an epoch changing work in the history of law-making. Because there are 18 chapters in which law has been discussed. The 14th of them about civil laws and remaining four about criminal laws and can be placed accordingly in these categories. Besides these only *Vyavahar Khand* of Katyayan is available also depicts the same picture and it seems to be entirely a book on civil laws. In this book process of law in detail has been described. Several scholars believe that *Puranas* contain only genealogies of *kshatriyas.* In these books, genealogies of *kshatriya* kings have been given. Many dynasties are considered to be fake ones; therefore, they cannot be relied upon. If we go through the inscriptions of post-Gupta period, we find that new kings began their dynasties from *Surya* dynasty and *Chandra* dynasty. These dynasties were not created by *kshatriyas* for themselves rather *Brahmins* created them. In lieu, therefore in *Brahmins* point of view of social history, it is necessary to read *Puranas.* Though there are 18 *Puranas* but amongst them *Vishnu, Brahmand, Bhagwat, Vayu, Matsya* and *Bhavishya* are considered ancient ones. Most of the *Puranas* were compiled by the end of Gupta period. But many *Puranas* continued to be written up to 15th and 16th century and corollaries kept on being inserted right up to 19th century. From social and cultural point of view *Agni Purana* has its own importance but it seems to have been written somewhere between 9th and 11th century. From economic point of view, we get some information about agriculture in *Agni Purana* which is just comparable to that of Brihat-Samhita of Varah Mihir (6th century) and Parasarsmriti (8th century).

Puranas are 18 in number. *Smritis* are told to be that much in number. At times, the number of castes and natures is also told to be 18. Just like this, there are 18 *Padas* traditionally which are used in various contexts. Therefore, it is not necessary that the numbers of *Puranas* are limited just to 18. *Puranas* have accommodated all kinds of subjects. Whatever knowledge, compilers had about society, religion, pilgrimages, and geography, ruling dynasties etc., all those have accommodated in *Puranas* and are found there. In most of the *Puranas,* many portions of *Dharmasastras* are found which helped in running social institutions. Compilers of Puranas' were not unaware of the concept of social changes.

They have described four *Yugas Satya, Treta, Dwapar,* and *Kali,* i.e., such of these Yugas have been considered inferior to the preceding era and it have been told that when after the end of one age there is advent of another age, the moral values and social standard declines. Thus, *Kali Yuga* has been told to be the age of cross-breeds (hybrids) during which age all people of all creeds and classes will put aside their duties designed according to *Shastra's* and will adopt another's occupation.

Main *Puranas* seemed to have been finally compiled around 400 AD. Two ancient epics namely the *Ramayana* and the *Mahabharata* are like *Puranas* only. *Mahabharata* are considered to be written by Vyasa. First of all there were only 8800 hymns (*shlokas*), it contained stories about victory and therefore, called Jaya Samhita. Later on, the hymns *(shlokas)* increased to 24000 and were named Bharata. It was called *Bharata* because it contained the story of the earliest Vedic *Jana Bharata's* predecessors. By the advent of Gupta period, the number of hymns increased to 1,00,000 hymns and this compilation was renamed *Mahabharata.* Its original story is a description of the battle between Kaurvas and Pandavas which was fought around 1000 BC during later Vedic period. The earliest social traditions discussed in this book can be utilised in the concept of the later Vedic period. But *Mahabharata* contains both descriptive and didactic parts. This part can be used in the contest of both post-Maurya and Gupta period. The *shantiparva* of the *Mahabharata* contains teaching about monarchy. The principles of levying tax propounded in this book, they are important from economic point of views. There are descriptions of *varnas* and castes. There are many hymns available in *shantiparva* which are available in Manusmriti word by word.

Ramayana is the treatise of Valmiki. Originally, there were 6000-which increased to 12000 and finally to 24000.

Compared to *Mahabharata,* this book is more homogenous about its subject. And there are not so many myths and stories. But here also preaching part has been added later on. Writing this book began most probably in 5th century BC, since then it has passed through five stages and its 5th stage seems to have continued up to 12th century. Taken together it seems, *Ramayana* was composed after *Mahabharata.* Those who want to know about patriarchal system of ancient India, for them it is important to go through *Ramayana.* Study of this book throws sufficient light on the conditions of women and *shudras.*

Some other literary works also throw sufficient light on economic and social status of this period. *Kamasutra* written by Vatsyayana is believed to be a work of Gupta period. Mainly this work is related to sexology. In this book, in one hand there is a clear description of luxurious life of people whereas on the other hand, landowners exploited the agricultural labourers and treated them as bonded labourers which is described to depict the thin exiting life of the people. According to R.K. Chaudhary by studying works of Vatsyayan, it seems that the writer was well aware of the geography and holistically divisions of the country and he had described different traditions and special customs practised in different parts of the country.[26]

As regards sources for study of Gupta period Kamandakiya Nitisar (400 AD to 800 AD) holds important place. The life of kings and their subjects have been described only in this book. Study of Kalidas's works is highly important to study Gupta period, if we believe Kalidas belongs to Gupta period. Through his works, he has portrayed the live sketch of contemporary economic life and his important works are Abhigyan Shakuntalam, Raghuvansham, Meghaduttam, Kumar Sambhavam, Malvikagnimitram, Ritusamhar, Vikramovar-shiyam. These important works of Kalidas provides vital aspects of Gupta period in details.[27] Kalidas had also provided India's well-geographical knowledge and he knew India the way a scholar geographer aware about *Bhagawatsharan* in his work "*Kalidas Kalin Bharat*-based on works of Kaildas produces a glimpse of the existing life.

When we follow the works of Kalidas, it looks as if he was not merely a poet but he viewed on social and economic systems also in a vivid and lively way. Kalidas, in his books described in details economic life of the society. From economic point of view also he described the rights and duties of the kings, different classes and varnas (castes). His book Raghuvansham is very important for studying agriculture and animal husbandry.

Besides the works of Kalidas, some other works of that period are also important to know about that period. They are Mrichhakatikam, written by Shudrak and Mudrarakshas and Devichandraguptam by Vishakhdatta. These books are mainly discussed on social aspects of that period.

Brihatsamhita (505-587 AD) which is completely a technical work in astrology throws sufficient light on contemporary tax levying arrangements.[28]

From this book of 6th century, we get enough knowledge also about the then existing agricultural processes and policies. Another famous book of Gupta period also a technical one is Namlinganushasan.[29] This book is also known as Amarkosh. This book has been written by Amar Singh. This is considered to be a great technical book. Seven types of uses of iron and two names of iron tools, extracted from iron alloy has appeared also in this book. The synonymous words mentioned in Amarkosh highlights the economic condition of that time. This book also mentions various occupations, tools and different types of apparatuses, used in varied purposes.

In order to know the economic life of India of Gupta period, the descriptions of Chinese pilgrims are- extremely important. Though, Fa-Hien, Huen Tsang were keenly interested know about the real essence of Buddhism and its practical importance in the society in that period, they were narrated certain things about administrative area. Fa-Hien visited India during the reign of Chandragupta-II (399 AD to 414 AD) and in his description he described about administrative system of Central Province i.e., modern days Uttar Pradesh and western Bihar. He also mention the mode of wage payment of kings to their servants and bodyguards.

But this Chinese visitor did not mention anything like this about Gupta king clearly as Huen Tsang told about Harsh Vardhan. He wrote about the common people and their social and economic conditions of that era. Whereas Fa-Hien most probably spent most of his time in studying to know about religious aspects and could only know very little about the life of the common men.

Lastly, the social condition of India in Gupta period was *Varna Vyavastha* i.e., caste system which was considered to be backbone and main corner stone of feudal tradition. In this connection, If we want to get a clear picture about the caste system and its evil practice, the first volume of Dr. Ambedkar's book could be seen an important study. Dr. Ambedkar realised that the caste system must be uprooted in India in view of giving them an equal status.

Dr Ambedkar wrote about the caste system in his book[30] since ancient time to modern time to highlight the untouchability and its negative impact on the society. In his work he also narrated about the exploitative and suppressive society for labouring classes divided into hundreds of castes which was brazenly for their aggrandizement by feudal lords which eventually made a serious impact in the lives of the peasants.

References

1. Christian Lassen, Indies Alteyar Tooms Kunde, Ramsharan Sharma, Prarambhik Bharat ka Arthik Avam Samajik Itihas, Delhi 1992, page-16.
2. Richard Fick, The social organisation in North East India in Buddha's Time, Calcutta, 1920, page-23.
3. Riz Davids, Notes on Early Economic Conditions in North India, London 1991, page-5.
4. N.C. Bandyophadhyay, Economic life and progress in Ancient India, Calcutta, 1945, page-52.
5. H.G. Rawlinson, Intercourse between India and western world, London 1916, page-19.
6. James Mill: History of India, 2 Volumes' London, 1820, page-155.
7. M.A Booch, Economic life in ancient Indian, Bombay, 1924.
8. N.C.Bandyopadhyay, referred earlier, page-75.
9. S.K. Das, Economic History of Ancient India, Calcutta, 1925, page-75.
10. Prananath: A Study in the Economic condition of Ancient India, Landon, 1924, page-89.
11. N.C. Bandyopadhyay, Arthik Iitihas ka Vidhivat Adhyayan, pp. 192-93.
12. U.N. Ghoshal, Hindu Revenue System in Ancient India, Calcutta 1929, page-31.
13. U.N. Ghoshal, The Agrarian System in Ancient India Calcutta 1990, page-101.
14. A.N. Bose Social and Rural Economy of Northern India, 2 Volumes, Calcutta 1952, page-95.
15. B.N. Dutta, Dialectics of Land Economics in India, Calcutta 1952, page-95.

16. D.D. Kosambi, An introduction to the study of Indian History, Bombay, 1956. And culture and civilisation of ancient India in Historical outline, Landon, 1965.
17. Devraj Chanana, Slavery in Indian, New Delhi 1960, page-56.
18. Ramsharan Sharma, Bharatiya Samantya Delhi, 1993, page-81.
19. D.N. Jha: Revenue System in Post-Mauryan and Gupta Times, New Delhi, 1977, Page-65.
20. S.K. Maity Economic life of Northen India in Gupta period, Delhi, 1970, Page-85.
21. M.H. Gopal Maury on Public Finance, New Delhi, 1989, Page-75.
22. Mazumdar and Altekar- Bhartiye Janata Kanaya Itihas, Page-86.
23. R.C. Mazumdar, A.D. Pusalkar (ed), History and culture of the Indian people, part-3. The classical Age Bombay, 1954, page-105.
24. Ramsharan Sharma referred above.
25. D.N. Jha referred above page-7
26. Radhakrishna Chaudhary, referred above.
27. Radhakrishna Chaudhary, referred above, Page-5.
28. D.N. Jha, referred above, page-19.
29. Amarkosh, edited by Harigovind Shastri Varanasi, 1968; 92, 98-99.
30. Bhimrao Amedkar, collection of writings and speeches, First volume (English), page-1-99.

1

Agriculture Order

In ancient India, circa 200 AD to 600 AD. or the period between the post-Maurya and the Gupta period is considered to be the period of rapid development of agriculture. State was making efforts to bring maximum area under cultivation and make them useful for yielding food grains. People were allotted land according to *Bhumichhidra Nyaya* and *Nividharma.*[1] In backward areas, *Brahmins* were granted sufficient cultivable land through land allotment grants in villages. During this period, personal rights on agricultural land were clearly envisaged. For religious purpose, inscriptions were found for the first time in north Bengal.[2] During Gupta period, inscriptions ordering purchase of uncultivated lands have been found again and again.[3] *Brahmins* had received land as *Agrahar* donation. Tendency to get land and increase landed property was increasing among the people. People were buying and selling land. Land related disputes got their birth out of this process. Keeping an eye on these disputes, the state administration made an elaborate arrangement for land distribution. Land distribution was done with the acceptance and through the village council. Land transfer was done with the approval of co-inhabitants and the approval of village council. Land transfer was done in the presence of village elders and its boundaries were marked.[4] According to Kamandak's *Nitisara* trade and farming was called "*Vartta*".[5] Raghuvansham describes them as the major source of national income.[6] Demand of cultivable land was on high priority. Narad made the arrangement that in case any owner died without leaving any heir or left for unknown destination for sometime then anyone could be allowed to cultivate his land. And on the return of the original landowner, he would be entitled to realise the cost of cultivation from him.[7]

In *Smritis,* farming had been considered to be the main occupation of *Vaishyas.* Land-ownership was mostly confined to them.[8] *Brahmins* had also received lots of land as *Agrahas* etc. And they also allotted lands by the order of the states. Though it could be assumed as a matter of conjecture.[9] The land-owners usually preferred to give their lands to the landless farmers and labourers for cultivation rather than they tilted their lands on their own and even they gave their lands to those people, who could plough and sow the seeds. In return, the peasant labourers ploughed and sowed for crops growing and received 35 to 50 per cent of produce from those land-owners.[10]

Very often land owning class used them as free-labour or bonded-labourer (*Begar*).[11] The system of *visti* (free-labour) was popular during that period.[12] Those who were entitled to exact *visti* they were normally used for farming works. A huge part of the society was tied to farming works as the cultivated lands were very fertile and reaped a rich harvest.[13]

There was very high-demand for residential and farming lands. Due to the lands given to *Brahmins-Purohits class,* many uncultivated and infertile lands got cultivated. But greedy *Brahmins* dumped them on the hands of wandering tribal peasants. As a result, their conditions got worsened to leave them in a state of hopelessness and despair to begin the trend of downwards in the society. On the other hand, in the tribal peasant areas of central India, greedy *Brahmins* who had received land grants and village grants on a large scale, got their fallow lands cultivated. This increased the tendency of converting fallow lands into cultivable land.[14] In later phases, kings donated forest land which is mentioned in the inscriptions available. In later days, *Shudra* made the arrangement that king should wave of land taxes of those who had dug out tanks and wells to help fallow lands conversion to cultivable land until they received double advantages compared to their investment.[15] In converting new land into cultivable land Buddhist beneficiaries of land grants and Brahmin and Jain and Buddha Sanghas worked a lot. Sages also produced grains to the possible extent, needed by them from the land adjoining their *Ashrams.*[16]

There are many instances related to officers, traders,,and artists wherein we traced evidences of their involvement in trades and other activities in their area to eke out their living.[17] According to Kamandak, in order to eke out their living, the peasants and landless labourers adopted the occupations of animal husbandry and agriculture and in trade-related activities the participation of *vaishyas* were seen.[18] Kamandak recommends that those in *Vratta*-type of occupations they should have the liberty to choose the profession according to their likings.[19] Kalidas wrote also that agriculture, animal husbandry etc are very important sources for revenue.[20] In post-Mauryan period in general and in Gupta period in particular as it is cleared from the works related to agriculture and there was a lot of development took place in the field of agriculture.[21]

Keeping in view the utility of fields, Narada has said if an owner of the agricultural field is unable to cultivate his land then in that case in the absence of the owner or anyone else if cultivated that field he will be entitled to the produce of that field.[22] Land cannot be kept fallow for indefinite period. In order to promote agriculture, the kings used to donate big chunks of cultivated land. Even the king waved off taxes and other charges to encourage tilting on the land as well. Such donees, donated the land to them, who were capable of turning them worth cultivating to set a new precedent in the form of tradition.

Even in forest areas, Brahmins were donated land to eke out their living and to organise education.[23] During the course of time, law-makers provided in the law that if someone establishes an industry or starts cultivation on a new allotted land or digs a well or tank therein and does something to develop in that land then king will have no right to impose any tax or ask anything till the time that particular person has recovered twice the invested amount towards profit.[24]

Due to development in the field of irrigation, agriculture got a big boost. Maximum part of the uncultivated land was converted into fertile agricultural lands. During those periods, peasants, Brahmins, Buddhists, and Jain Sangas had cleared forests and bushes and made them habitable and cultivable.[25] Besides common peasants, and family men, amongst Brahmins, Buddhist and religious sect agriculture was the main occupation and made rapid stride. According to Kalidas, the produce raised by the inhabitants of that area from lands cultivated by them was used for the management of *ashrams*.[26] There was stringent punishment prescribed against the theft of food grains from the farm houses and the agricultural lands.[27] From Brihaspati's works it is known that the thief will have to repay ten times the amount theft to the inhabitants of the Ashrams and to the owners of the land. Even the capital punishment was prescribed, when any person takes away grass, wood, fruits, and flowers etc and appreneded in that case his hands should be chopped off.[28] Any person who has stolen grains 10 times of kumbha should be awarded death punishment in case it is less than 10 kumhas, 11 times of the quantity stolen should be realised towards punishment and his entire property should be handed over to the owner.[29] Brihaspati has also said that one who commits theft he will be awarded minimum punishment of 100 panas or even more which will be commensurate with his crime.[30]

If one plucks someone else's fruits, uproots tree or cuts it from root very strong punishment were given. If someone's cattle harmed the field of another person, owner of the cattle was punished severely. If the field is not fenced well by barriers, the punishment was reduced. Similar was the case of fields that were located adjacent to the roads. If the field was only trampled under feet the punishment was proportionately reduced. Farm owners paid proper wages to the labourers. But where wages were undecided, farm labourers were entitled to 1/10th of the farm produce towards wage.[31] According to Narad, if any one destroys fruits, roots, sources of water, agriculture implements, he should be declared culprit of 1st grade.[32]

It was common practice for the farmers to fence their fields.[33] If someone's cattle cross the fence and harm the crop the cattle owner should be punished and he should be cautioned. But if the crop has been destroyed with its roots, the owner can award grain as punishment to the cattle tender which will be paid by his master.[34] The king may levy a tax for one or two months. By applying above mentioned punishments it seems that the agriculture labour was treated as the weakest class. By the gravity of punishment also it seems that grain was rare. Land and produce was controlled by the land owners. King could cultivate on donated land but he could not interfere with the residence and living standard of the subjects.[35] According to details available from the copper inscriptions of Dharsen-IInd from Mali. No body should hinder the use of land donated to Brahmins after two centuries in the Alina copper inscriptions Shiladitya seventh; we find similar laws about the villages.[36]

Kalidas has termed it as a source of national prosperity. Because agriculture was the backbone of economy, therefore, agricultural development was given highly emphasised. From his writings, it is known that even sages cultivated the land around their *ashrams* to eke out their livelihood.[37] Because of development in the field of irrigation, the yielding in the agriculture also enhanced. According to Fa-Hien, agriculture was the main occupation of the rural people which witnessed a gradual growth.[38] Forests were cleared and new farm lands were created. Water was drained out from low-lying lands and agriculture became increasingly important. The interest shown by the state in cultivating land and convert forest land into cultivable land and thus showing interest in agriculture and other allied things boosted the growth in this man area.

Narad[39] and Brihaspati[40] have formulated laws for big land labourers. Amongst them three types of labourers were available on rent and the position of agricultural-labourers was in the middle. Brishastiati has categorised them in three categories according to the share of produce or wages they received in farming in terms of grain producing i.e.,low, middle and high. Those who worked in the field were provided 1/5th of produce besides food. But where it was based only on wage they received 1/3rd of the produce. But those who did not complete the works of the masters, given to them were not paid wages.

During Gupta period, land got enough fragmentation. A village farmer owned only a small plot of land which he and his family cultivated.[41] Descriptions are available about big land owners well such as in the Gunaidhar Patra. There is descriptions of a man owning about 11 *patakas*[42] of land. Here land-owner for the purpose of agriculture had hired bonded-labourers and used them in cultivation through share croppers. For land-owners and bonded-labourers Narad[43] and Brihaspati[44] have propounded laws regarding imposition of taxes and their wages. When the amount of wage is not fixed agriculture labourer could receive the amount of wage up to 10th of the produce.[45] Implements required for agriculture were provided by the land owners. Agriculture labourers were supported to take enough care of those tools.[46] If agricultural labourer is unable to work despite receiving wages, he will have to pay double of the received amount as punishment to the master.[47] In those days, bonded-labourers were of three types, cultivators' utensil makers and common peasants who came from middle class.[48]

Brihaspati on the basis of their share in land produce has categorised agriculture labourers into three different categories– high, middle and low.[49] According to Brihaspati, land-owners should give a third or fifth share to them towards their share.[50] Those labourers, who took their food and clothes from their masters for working they were given one-fifth of the produce but in cases where he worked without receiving food and clothes, he received one-third of the total produce.[51] Brihaspati had made several laws in favour of land owners. If any labourers left even the smallest part of the work unfinished, he had to forego his entire wages. For this crime, he could even be produced in the court of law.[52] If any labourer despite receiving wages did not turn up to work while remaining physically fit he had to pay back twice the amount of wage to the king as punishment and return the wages to his master.[53]

Commonly, the lands could be divided into two categories: cultivable and non-cultivable. Each type of crop could not be cultivated on every type of land. Such land which received enough rainfall were worthy for cultivation. Eastern UP, Bihar, and Bengal etc., and plain lands of Gangetic valley were such lands. Another type of land were fit for the cultivation of barley, wheat, maize etc., i.e. Sindh, Rajasthan and Punjab.

In order to receive high yields of various crops sufficient quantity of water was required, therefore many artificial methods of irrigations were adopted.

Mostly cultivation works was carried out by the most common agricultural labourers.[54] However according to Brihaspati, agricultural works should be carried out by capable and most hard-working labourers.[55] But in case of shortage of cattle and seeds, people combined together to cover-up the shortage and complete the work.[56] On account of disease, famine or natural calamities land used to shift to some influential hands. But as regards elder of the family, Brihaspati and Narad opine that some parts should be received by him along with that the rest should be described among all the family members.[57] It looks within only a few generations huge part of land got fragmented into small pieces of land. According to A.L. Bhasam, in ancient India very big land owners as a big class are not seen.[58]

Land-ownership

Based on literary sources and inscriptions, we get to know about various theories about land ownership, there were three types of land-ownership in this period, individual or personal land-ownership, state land-ownership, and co-operative land-ownership.[59] There is a general saying that land belongs to one, who cleared the forest first, a deer belongs to one who hunted it down and this is true also.[60] But here the theory of land and deer do not seem to go true in practical life. Because on dead, there will arise dispute within the group and about permanent ownership of the land as well and dispute will raise its head again. Initially, because there was agricultural land in plenty and they used land for cultivation according to their requirement. The main reason behind this was the demand of land was considerably less as there was very limited population. But when the life began along with agriculture and population started growing, land disputes started beginning quite naturally. Land could not be allowed to use without proper proof for long time.

S.K. Maity says that with the changing time without legal-base, permanent ownership of land was not considered properly by the Indian society.[61] Many law-givers opposed temporary ownership of the land and made laws to provide them legal status. According to Yagyavalkya, without legal proof claim on land is not proper.[62] It is valid only with legal proof. According to Brishaspati, only that claim is valid which is corroborated by sufficient evidences.[63] Narad's opinion in this respect differs from the rest. Use of land without sufficient and adequate proof is improper. Proof is necessary for this. In such a situation, temporary right is not just sufficient. Yet according to Brihaspati, just this one proof does not give land over real right on the land. Narad has mentioned a number of laws passed against illegal ownership of land. According to him, without adequate proof of land, one who claims the land should be considered as a thief.[64] If someone keeps control of land for even over hundred years and used those land without having sufficient proof in the capacity of a owner he should be punished as a thief[65] but this law has been struck down by Narad himself and Brihaspati as well.

Narad and Brishaspati have made other laws also for proper maintaining of ownership of land. If someone keeps his control over any land without any objection of anybody for over thirty years, in that case this property cannot be taken back from him. In such a situation, even the real owner will also lose his property.[66] At one place, this also has been said that land, house and other property, if that have been used by someone else, the owner cannot lose that even if the user may be his friend, relative or his own brother.[67] But in case of such a property is in the possession of his son-in–law, or any educated *Brahmin,* king or his ministers, in that case even after long gap of time it cannot become their legal property.[68] In this way, any property under the possession of third generation it gets transferred to fourth generation, then their legal rights are established on them and no proof can be asked therefore in respect of the same.[69] Any property which has not been snatched and has remained under his possession for a long time then in such cases he will be legal owner of that property.[70]

Narad *Smriti* also supports this view. Despite having long-time possession of the land as a criterion of ownership, legal experts have themselves emphasised on its inadequacy and expressed that without legal right the ownership of the land is not possible.[71] Yagyavalkya has written that if any land owner has obtained legal validity then his ownership of that land will be recognised.[72] Without obtaining that it is not recognised as legally valid. The opinion of Brihaspati is also similar to this.[73] Narad has said that anyone claiming right of the land without showing valid documents, the legal right of that land should certainly be treated as a thief and in that case the ruler of that area will decide his punishment which is deemed fit.[74] According to S.K. Maity, Narada and Brihaspati have rebutted this law.[75] They only consider long-time possession of land as the only criterion for land ownership.[76] Generally, long-time possession of land as a criterion for land ownership was popular in the under-developed parts of the country. Where the situation was comparatively less developed and it was considered to be legal right of the land on the basis of long-time possession of the land.[77] Yagyavalkya made some amendments which is agreeable on possession of the land.[78] On the face of it, actual criteria of the land ownership will be decided on the basis of a fixed period and that has been increased the length of time from 10 to 20 years. According to Yagyavalkya, use of land forcefully was unacceptable even with proof.[79] Thus, possession on land should not be the sole criteria of legal right[80] and legally validity is also equally important to decide the legal ownership of the land.[81]

According to S.K. Maity, the idea of possession of land as first right was only practically possible when demand for land was not very high.[82] In the subsequent period, when the demand for land shot up due to rapid development in the crops production, the legal experts framed a number of laws to address these perennial problems. With this the challenge posed on the titles of the land owners resolved to a great extent as it provides a good measure to recognise the right of the land owner. Many provisions were also made to implement it in a proper way. For that a strong administrative power in connivance with the ruler of the place for equal development is very essential. This was the reason why king was considered to be the as the son of god. Brihaspati has also said that king is the master of all.[83]

During Gupta period, this form of ruling by the king is considered to be above all the things because king in principle was accepted as master of everything. Therefore, such legal arrangements were also made in such a way that the ruler of the area could be in a position to donate the land and villages to Brahmins to execute the religious acvities and later becomes master of that donated lands or villages. This could not be possible until the king was not accepted as the real master of land. The copper plate inscriptions of this period where in village donation and land donations are described these issues. The copper plate inscription of Gaya and Nalanda of Samaudra Gupta, Bhitari cave inscription of Skanda Gupta,

Raipur copper plate inscription of Mahasukdeoraj, Shivani copper plate inscription of Pravarasen-IInd, Karidalai copper plate inscription of Jaynath, cave inscription of Jaynath etc.,[84] are important Donation inscription issued by the state make it amply clear that in principle, king was the owner of entire land, although on a very large scale the practice of private/individual ownership on land might have practically been existing, otherwise, he could not have donated the villages in this way. In such cases, the donees were not only collecting administrative taxes but were also using them but this has never been said that they had the right to disposes the peasants of their rights to punish them.

According to Yagyavalkya, the king accepts one-sixth of the produce by providing legally adequate protection to his subjects. If he realises taxes from them without providing such protection in that case he earns half of sin committed by the subject.[85] The responsibility of the king was to protect his subjects. This contention was logically carried to such logical conclusion that law books like Vishnu *Smriti,*[86] and Yagyavalkya[87] *Smriti* have almost been expected of the king that in case he fails to find out the stolen property, he should give equal amount of property to him. These all indicates the same thought that taxes were realised in place of the services rendered by the king or the state.[88]

According to SK Maity, the new owner of the land could neither make any relaxation in the tax nor impose any new tax.[89] If he did so, he deserved punishments.[90] Donee had no right to discourage or encourage the peasants to pay taxes to the state. He had no right to take back the land from peasants or establish possession over the donated village. According to Fleet, in order to purchase or donate any land common citizens had to take permission from the state.[91] Under no situation, it was necessary for the state to interfere in the transference of common property because no proof of such interference has been found from this period.[92] Thus, king or his ancestors had no right over donated land. But in certain cases to seize this property or to give it to someone-else was the prerogative of the king. According to the legal provisions in *Smriti's* king could take possession of the properties of those, who died without leaving any heir.[93] This statement has been supported by Brihaspati[94] and Narada[95] both. According to them, if any *Kshatriya, Vaishya or Shudra* dies without leaving any male child, wife or brother, his property should be taken to possession by the king, because, he is the master of all. royal ownership. It is proved by this fact that the king used various types of taxes realised in his own interest. According to Narada and other early *Dharmashastra* writers, it is seen that almost sixth part of the crop produce was a payment to be made to the king or ruler by the subjects in lieu of getting protection as the king is duty-bound to protect the interst of the subjects.[96] This is again substantiated by several literary evidences.[97] Kalidas wrote that the property of the subjects is protected from dacoits and thieves by the king. Obviously, it is important that the king is made owner of the sixth part of the produce.[98]

According to SK Maity, perhaps king possessed the ownership some land directly under his control. Huen Tsang had also written that in central India people lived a very happy life due to good governance of king as they did not have to appear before any officer of the state to use their land. Only those people had to pay a part of the produce to the ruler, who worked on the land of the state.[99] There are several instances of the sale and purchase of the state land, we get descriptions of them.[100] State had the monopoly only on the minerals dug-out of the land, without any doubt. Prior to this rule, according to Vishnu *Smriti,* the property found by digging, half belonged to the king, because he was the protector and master of the land.[101]

According to Damodarpur, copper-plate inscription undivided plate 'B', plate 'C' and Plate 'A' indicate private ownership, joint ownership and combined ownership respectively.[102] Personal ownership was given under certain restrictions, if its owner wanted to dispose it, he could not directly transfer it to the purchaser, and rather this process was to be done in the presence of village elder under his influence. The process of transfer of land in each case was to be done in the presence of the village.[103] P.V. Kane also supports this statement. According to him, cultivators had the right on fertile lands and king used to be only a share-holder of a part of the produce.[104] Fallow land was possessed by the king. According to this rule even if all fertile lands were not cultivated by someone those lands are considered to be the royal property. In this way, royal property which consisted of both fallow and fertile lands were under direct control of the king, over and above that, in lieu of protection related services rendered by the ruler, he received taxes on a regular basis which shows his indirect control over even personal land.[105]

According to Campbell[106] and Mane,[107] mutually village community owned the land jointly. Fleets find a symbol of a type of community ownership in the Maliye Copper plate inscription of Dharsen-II,[108] whereas on the other hand, R.G. Basak supports community ownership of the villagers on the land. But, here, the question arises, if the land was under the exclusive control of the king, why the king did not sale it[109] independently and rather it was done through village elders or trading class and at time by the entire people on the ruler's disposal. Why in cases of lands without any definite tax and fallow land the government did not take upon itself directly the transfer of these land. Perhaps land were related to entire Gram Sabhas or the entire village rather than that of the state.[110] Therefore consent of entire village was taken rather than that of the state. Therefore, the consent of the entire village was taken for the transfer of these lands. No land could be sold either by the state or by the village elders alone. For this purpose, the due approval of both king and subjects were necessary. By producing one proof this point gets all the more clear.[111] Therefore, land was neither owned by the state nor by the Gram Sabhas, it belonged to the peasants working on them and state realised 1/6th of them only as taxes. R.C. Majumdar and A.S. Altekars also support Bassak views on this aspect. According to Majumdar, real owner of the village land used to be village *Samitis.* These *Samitis* used to be responsible for the payments of entire taxes levied by the state. If any person was unable to repay the taxes of his land and was considered to be the property of the village *Samitis.* They had the right to sale with the purpose of repaying the taxes by the *Samitis*.[112] In the same way, Altekar states that on cultivable land, individual or family had the ownership rights and not of the state.[113]

According to S.K. Maity, transfer of land to new owners was important for the villagers. Therefore, through the village elders with the concurrence of the thoughts of the villages, new owners were made aware because they used to be well-aware of the boundaries of the village land and other facets. Mostly, disputes regarding landed property were solved with the opinion of the respected people of the village and their decision on the matter and land ownership was accorded stability.[114] This opinion of Basak has also been supported by Mazumdar.[115] But D.N. Jha has not supported Basak, opinion. According to him, Basak's argument was not logical. Because transfer of land and arrival of new land owner was such a matter, that evidently was related to entire village and therefore, through prominent people of the village and their concurrent opinion was considered important.[116] Besides these, in case of boundary disputes, neighbours and elderly people importance was even accepted by the legal books. According to Manu, fields, tanks, orchards, boundaries of the houses-maps problems related to these depended on the basis of the witness.[117] A similar view is referred by Yagyavlkya which can also be cited.[118] Similarly, according to Narada's decision regarding land disputes depend on the opinion of neighbours, the inhabitants of same city or village, other people of the same community and elder people of the same village.[119] Brihaspati has also accepted the importance of neighbours, elderly inhabitants.[120] Besides these it has also been said that any person acceptable to both the sides can also decide the boundary.[121]

K.P. Jayaswal has described personal ownership of land on the basis of several principles.[122] But UN Ghoshal[123] and A.L. Basam[124] have opposed this principle. According to Ghosal, the three examples cited by Jayaswal to show that king had no right on the land, In fact, they proved that they have the opposite ownership of land was sometimes decided by obeying certain laws. For example, (a) Nividharma,[125] (b) Akshay Nividharma[126] or Akshay Nivi, (c) Nividharma Akshaya[127] (d) Apaddha Dharma[128] (e) Apaddhakshaya or Nividharma[129] or Apaddhakshaya Nivisama Maryada, and (f) Bhumi Chhidranyaya.[130] Various historians have analysed Nivi and Nividharma in various manners. Jayaswal says that nivi was a fiscal word of Hindu administrative system which means written forms documents' on different works and laws. This kind of above mentioned description makes it clear that land ownership which was with the king in Mauryan period remained so up to some length of post-Maryan period. But during Gupta period, lot of important changes took place. During this period, all the three types of land ownership such as personal, royal and community ownership can be seen and their examples are available. Though during the course of time, there was growth in the tendency of personal land ownership and the king was left with only land revenue.

So far as land labourers are concerned, regarding this Amarkosh has used the word *"visti"* which is a synonym of *"Aju"* it was used for Korby labour. *Visti* is known in Hind as "Begari". Moniar Williams has translated it as bonded-labour. According to *Agnipuranaa,* king had to arrange for their food those who were used as bonded-labour.

During Gupta period, generally small farmers were there, who ploughed their fields along with their family but at certain places in the inscription of Gunaidhar, there is mention of eleven *patakas* of land. In the same way, such big lands which were donated were cultivated by land-based labourers. According to Narada and Brishaspati, servants ploughing land were paid either in cash or 1/5th of the produce. And such servants who did not take food, clothes were given one-third of the produce. This way, landless labourers could get their livelihood respectfully. But during the course of time, their condition became worst to worsening.

Knowledge of Agriculture

In various *Smriti* books, Brihat Samhita written by Varah Mihir and Amarkosh written by Amarsingh, there are detailed description of various aspects of agriculture. In these days, people then surviving on the making of ploughing tools and process of preparing field for cultivation. These tools are being used in agriculture, process of thrashing, ploughing the field, and in various grain and fruit seeds and their transplantation. Moreover, their appropriate time and methods, diseases of plants and their cure, condition of good fields, various crops and yields and types of crops are described in such details that we get to know and learn about them a lot.

Through Brihatsamhita, we know the finer details and description of contemporary agriculture processes. Fields were ploughed with the help of plough share and oxen[131] after ploughing the field bunds were made.[132] For good crops seeds were sown on time after keeping the time of rainfall in mind and[133] after the crops riped within a specific period,[134] the grans were extracted through the process of thrashing. Food grains were separated from husk in air and thus grains were accumulated.[135] But paddy was stored along with husk.[136] In those days, mainly two types of crops were sown that was before rains[137] and after rains, which can be termed as *old Kharif* and *Rabi crops*. Before rains paddy was cultivated which was harvested during winter?[138] Post-grain crops included wheat and barley which used to get ready in summer season.[139] Varahmihir has described about spring season[140] crops which were cultivated in the months of Shrawana, Chaitra and Vaishak Nakshatras.[141]

According to Brihatsamhita, the selection of fields were very important for good harvest for particular crops.[142] If there is flow of water under top soil, it will destroy even good crops. Later on, he has said if the level of under-ground water is four hands down (Six feet), it will stop the growth of the plant to destroy them and even even stopped the process of developing plants.[143]

According to Brihatsamhita, during Gupta period there were nine types of paddy crops i.e., Shali,[144] Kalamshal,[145] Yavaka,[146] Sukraka,[147] Shashatika,[148] Rakla Sali,[149] Panduka,[150] Gaurashali[151] and Nishpawa.[152] Besides barley[152] and wheat,[154] Kodrawa[155] and Kanga[156] were other type of crops. There were six types of pulse crops i.e., Moong,[157] Maska,[158] Mashoor[159] Kulthi,[160] Vailay,[161] and Onka.[162] There were three types of oilseeds namely, Til,[163] Sarspha,[164] and Siddharth.[165] Besides these there were cotton, jute, lentil and sugarcane crops were also culivated. Kodo and Kongu were also grown by poor and landless peasants for their own consumption which shows economic disparity of those days. It was evident that the then farm labourers were susrviving by working in the large fields which are the result of uneven distribution of land in the society.

Interesting information related to agriculture is available in Brishatsamhita written by Varahmihr. He had forecasted seven types of destructions which caused enormous damage to crop growers and farmers and two happy times for them also. In Brihatsamhita, forecasts about flood, famine, drought, and economic downfall have also been made. Here, in too much of rain and scanty of rainfall have been described as the causes of famine. In the Junagarh inscription of S. Kanda Gupta, due to very heavy rain Sudarshan said, the rivers overflowed causing flood which caused destruction and devastation very clearly from the point of view of agricultural peasants depending farming on rains very often suffered from the dangers of flood and drought. Another important point was that due to the scarcity of rainfall, the crops growing was not only affected seriously but it also led to deforestation.

In Brishaspati Samhita, we find description of 255 types of plants;[166] also we get to know how to prepare soil for planting these plants. According to Varahmihir, growing sesame trees on the field is another way to improve the fertile quality of the soil. These soft trees have to grow and thereafter chopping and mixing them with the soil as it serves a good purpose in the form of very good fertiliser. He has also mentioned how grafting can be done and another plant can be raised in jack fruit, ashok banana, lemon, pomegranate, grape, papaya, large sweet lemons, jasmine, grape vine etc., in different categories from which. Varahmihir has also suggested time and season for grafting and taking out graft.

Requirements and use of different types of soil for different crops and plants have also been described in Brihatsamhita. Eugenia, vyas, manira, large seed lemon, lemon, pomegranate, jack fruit need damp soil.[167] Fixed distant are between one tree to another tree should be 20 hand (30 ft) and they should be sown 16 hands (24 feet). If the trees are planted without giving such type of gap then the fruition will not be good because their branches will come close to each other to affect their growing and production.

During those days, peasants used to grow several types of crops like Rabi and Kharif which can be grown in different seasons. Amarakosh provides a counts of crops grown in those days these are wheat, paddy, jowar, sugarcane, bazra pea, pulse, til, mustard, lentil, ginger, black pepper etc.[168] Besides these various types of vegetables and medicinal plants were grown in those days which are described in agriculture. Raghuvansh written by Kalidas described several types of paddy in nivada, shali and kalam.[169] One of the varieties mentioned in Amarkosh can be grown in only 60 days.[170]

S.K. Maity has described Kalama, Niyura, Achachadhan, Shali, Shyam varieties of paddy is mentioned, which were grown in those days. Both the systems i.e., direct broadcasting and transplantation methods were in used in those days but the best crops were raised by transplantation method only. One more important rabi crop was wheat. Though there is no apparently obvious description of wheat in epics, but in Ganapath this word is available.[171] In later this has become very popular crop in food production.

From contemporary literary sources, it is known that during this period several types of vegetables were also grown. Main vegetables described in Amarkosh are cucumber, onion, garlic, pumpkin etc. During this period sugarcane was also grown. The proofs of these crops grown are available since Vedic period.[172] Megasthenese and Diodorus have described the sweetness of sugarcane juice.[173] Starbo has described sugarcane as honey plant. During Gupta period, cultivation of sugarcane crop and co-operation had developed to a great extent.[174] Amarkosh states that sugar was extracted from sugarcane juice.[175] During this period, fibrous plant like cotton was cultivated mainly. Unlike wild cotton plants, cotton was cultivated in cotton fields, specially prepared for cotton cultivation like other crops besides this cultivation of ganza and jute is also described.

In the writings of Kalidas journey descriptons of Huen Tsang and in Amarkosh, there is description of Saffron cultivation. All three of them have described the cultivation of spices, black pepper, cardamom cloves and beside these sandals and in the plains of Malaya. Malaya is the southern part of western *ghat*. During the day of Kalidas, it was known as a part of pandya country, today it is a part of Kerala.

During those days, even from forests and orchards several types of fruits were harvested. Prominent among them are toddy fruits, oranges, pomegranates, grapes, coconut, dates, mangoes, pine apple, wild berry etc. Mango was the most important fruit which is provides and coconut was also the second most important fruit which is proved by contemporary literature.[177] Cosmos has described coconut as fruit which is sweet and pleasant to eat.[178]

It was cultivated mainly in Bengal, Orissa and coastal areas of Madras and Kerala. Even beatle was cultivated in these areas. Some fruits like oranges and pomegranates were mainly cultivated in Assam, Darjeeling, Nagpur and Kashmir in the hilly areas. Pine apples, mango, banana etc grew in Bihar, Odissa, Bengal and Assam.

Thus, during the post-Maurya to Gupta period, agricultural knowledge was imparted very well amongst the farmers for food production. During those days, all even food crops were grown which were able to maintain and sustain their importance in the past and thereafter as well. Along with this keeping in mind, the type of lands (soil) crops suited to the nature of these lands were grown on them. Consequently, agricultural production has got a big boost.

Agricultural Techniques

With the gradual development in civilisation, practical experience and regularly developing innovative techniques heralded a new impetus to agricultural production and that of course after the proper application of these methods. Iron is being one of the strongest and sharpest metals, proved to be very useful for agriculture. Main agricultural implements like plough share, sade pickaxes, sickle etc have been in use from Vedic period with little changes and enrichment. But with the passing time and situation changes kept on coming in these tools as per their necessity. The farmers also according to their needs and knowledge invented some new forms of tools for easy and suitable use.[178]

Most important agricultural implement was ox-driven plough. For good agricultural produce, land was ploughed well made and made light, smooth and useful for crops growing. According to Parashar, a plough had eight parts (a) Isa (b) Jua (c) Niryola (d) Niryota (e) Pasika (f) Halasthonu (g) Adyachala and (h) Shaula Pachhani.[179] According to Amarkosh, important parts of a plough were bar of the beam pen of the beam share etc.[180] Peasants almost used iron spear. According to *Brihaspati,* a spear weighing 12 pals should be brought in use.[181] According to cosmos, some people used hide of hippopotamus[182] in place of iron though such descriptions are not available anywhere else. Number of oxen used in the plough is not mentioned anywhere. In later period, Shukra mentions that Brahmins should use 16 *kshatriyas,* 12 *vaishyas,* and four *shudras* or untouchables in two bullocks.[183] In a society, it has divided on the basis of caste and nature of works.

As per present concurrent thoughts of the time use of two bullocks in a plough is coming down from centuries, but in ancient Buddhist literature *Suttanipat,* plough driven by 10-12 bullocks is described.

Spade and pick axe were the second most important agricultural[184] tool was put into practice after plough. Spade was used to dig hard soil and prepare the left over soil after ploughing particularly on corners and sides. Other implements used were sickle, musal (wooden pastle), ikhalee (mortar) soop (winnowing basket) dhanyakrit seive etc.[185] During harvest of the crop these implement of the tools have been mentioned several times.[186] From the harvested crop to separate grains either sticks were used or bullocks were used by blowing the grains with a soop the husk was removed and grains separated.[187]

Except a few modern scientific and technical equipments and knowledge of almost other tools used in agriculture, the Indian farmers use them in plenty in grain production which of course were suits during those days. During this period, use of implements accompanied with use of variety of agricultural processes in India has left enough proof available today. Some of these are ploughing in the field, broadcasting seeds, weeding, irrigation, plant protection, harvesting thrashing, blowing, storing grains, methods of preparing rice and flour.[188]

The question of agriculture equipments is tied with the changes on earth. From Mauryan period to downfall of Gupta period, the land was tilled and ploughed in the same was as result of which earth has been turning up and down between one to one and half-feet only. This shows that there has been no qualitative change in the agricultural tools. During Maurya period, the efforts made by state was very ambitious to convert fallow land and forests into cultivable land due to such works and effects not only Gangetic land but Narmada and in south up to Godavari; the land had become cultivable Kaveri valley of Karnataka also had become familiar to agricultural implements of Mauryan period.

During this entire period the plough, share-fitted with them the number of bullocks in them spades for digging the soil and sickles to crop the plant for harvesting, these three implements amongst themselves lead the agricultural revolution which were sheltered by the peasants of Mauryan period and for centuries due to agricultural practices they remained as leaders during Mauryan period i.e., during the times of Buddha 12 to 16 bullocks drawn ploughs were in use, because that was the first occasion to ring fallow lands and hard soils under plough it was initial attempt. At state level, intensive ploughing of land and broadcasting seeds initiated by Mauryan and this initiative worked and continued in Shunga period Kusahan period continued up to entire Gupta period. During Kushana period, no changes were expected. The central Asian area where from they came, for them Indian land at that time easy passing through a revolution and they took pride in just inheriting it and its continuance. Guptas were original inhabitants of India and during their period as well no changes came in which could be said qualitative in agriculture-related equipments in Brihatsamhita written by Varahmihir. Yet, therein is the description of season, rain, drought, harvest, broadcasting seeds, protections of seeds, protections of grains and other facts necessary for agricultural operations which are very useful compilations. Thus, in this period we do not find any mention of scientific finding of implements used for agricultural operations.

From literary sources (*Atharva veda, Arthashastra* etc), it is evident that from ancient times itself, Indian farmers knew the use of manure and they used them. During post-Mauryan period just like Maurya period dung, bone fishes etc were continuously used as fertilisers in the field. During this period in distant north-western areas, farmers used fertilisers in their fields and harvested very good crops as a result.[189] According to classical writers, huge plain areas of India were highly fertile.[190] In those fields, maize, pulses, rice and other food crops were grown in plenty. From this, it is clear that despite presence or absences of organised or scientific fertiliser systems popularity it is definite that peasants used some kind of fertiliser and as a result surplus production could be made possible. A Chinese description of third century AD describes that Indian soil is extremely fertile.[191] *Ramayana*[192] also says that Kosal Magadha and Vats' area are very rich in respect of crops. In this way, fertiliser was used to keep the fertility of land and production maintained in post-Mauryan period.

In post-Mauryan period, crop-cycle and mixed cropping was adopted. According to season, different crops were raised in those days as components of fertilizer Sesamum Seed (Fil) grinded barely, meat etc are also found mentioned in literary[193] sources of Gupta period such as *Agnipurana*[194] *and* Brihatsamhila[195] etc., sufficient use of fertiliser is found mentioned.[196] Fertilizer was prepared from dung of cows, goats and sheeps and other animals and grasses rotten in water. Brihatsamhita and *Agnipuran* describes that compost fertiliser was prepared from pulses, sesamum plant, barley, goat, sheep and animal dung, fish, animal hides and fats.[197]

In *Aginpuran,* there is description of other fertilizers also such as cod fish water for mango, for dates and coconuts salted water and for all trees fish and sweet water and there is also description of directing how to irrigate trees i.e, in summer both in morning and evening in winters once in two days and in rainy season, when soil is dry. In Brihatsamhita forms of seeds, various measures for their germination are mentioned.

Irrigation Arrangements

A country like India, affected by monsoon depended mainly on irrigation for agriculture in order to increase the productivity personal as well as state level efforts have continuously been made to irrigate plots. As various sources of irrigation in ancient India in different areas rivers, canals, lakes, tanks, wells etc have been discussed in contemporary literature and archaeological sources.

In post-Mauryan India, the importance of irrigation is known through several sources in one hymns of *Adiparwa* it has been said.

That one tank is hundred times more important than[198] a well, it is mentioned in Manusmriti that boarder between two villages should be decided by tanks or other water sources.[199] Behind this the motive of Manu was to provide irrigation facility for that village which could be possible through that water. In other *Smriti* books there is a description of stringent punishment, who tries to damage the water dams. Manu talks to sink him in water until death or head to be chopped.[200] Vishnusmriti provides economic punishment for this.[201] Such provisions clearly indicate importance of community, utility of tanks and other water dams.

Archaeological excavations at Hastinpur[202], New Delhi[203], Ropar[204], Ujjain[205], Mathura[206] and Nasik[207] have discovered many fenced wells of post-Mauryan period which indicates that farmers of those days were provided with the facility of irrigation. Wells found in the excavations of historical sites of eastern UP and Bihar to what extent were utilised, it is different to says. According to R.S. Sharma, main purpose of these wells was no irrigation.[208] The basis of his saying is that for the purpose of irrigation wells should have been located in the middle of cultivable land but according to the description of Patanjali, these wells were used for irrigation.[209] Besides this arrangement for the storage of water for irrigation were made at individual group and state-level during this period. By the description available in Manusmriti, it is clear that it was the responsibility of villages to protect and safeguard[210] such water bodies several evidence are available about the construction of tanks in post-Mauryan period. Several such evidences have been found from north western provinces. The keen interest taken by the king and state in the construction, development and protection of the sources of irrigation is supported by archaeological evidences also. Mathura stone inscription of Shaka ruler Sodas supports the construction of tank, storage mechanism.[211] Many such tanks have been found by the digging at Taxila, Hastinapur, Koshambi, Bhitta and Besnagar.

It is clear by the state supported individual efforts that lots of wells and water body mechanisms were constructed but to what extent these were used for the purpose of irrigation is very difficult to say. This is also the opinion of historian G.L. Adya.[212] On the basis of epigraphy Shyam Sundar Nigam opines that ruling class took enormous interest in the construction and development of means of irrigation on the basis of literary sources.[213] Beni Prasad opines that providing irrigational facilities were one of the main responsibilities of the king. Therefore, this can be inferred that during this period peasants were provided both types of irrigation facilities by the state.

Rulers of Gupta period recognised the importance of irrigation in the development of agriculture. Proof of provision of irrigation facilities to the peasants is available in literature and inscriptions. In the opinion of Kamandak, for the welfare and development of peasants, they were lesser dependence on rains and maximisation of irrigation facilities was felt necessary.[214] *Smriti* writer Narada has described water system into two parts khep, and bound.[215] The water system developed by digging earth was called khep, whereas to protect the fields from water to build bunds or embankments and thus to protect the irrigational facilities. About this Narada says any person with the permission of the owner could rejuvenate or reconstruct the water system or embankment or bunds otherwise, he had no right to interfere.[216] But in case of the death of the owner, he could do so with the permission of the state or the king.[217] According to Brihaspati *smriti* anyone damaging the embankment could be punished up to 100 panas or even more depending on his tendency towards crime.[218] Similar description is available from Amarkosh that a canal is dug from a river or tank and these were taken to distant places.[219] Jalanirgam word which is available in literature is synonyms for canal or drain. It is mentioned that such Jalanirgam or drains protected from overflowing of water;[220] "Dirghika word has been used for community irrigating as well as for drinking purposes.[221] The word is meant a very huge tank and this word has also been used by Kalidas in his book Malavikagnimitram.[222] In Amarkosh, such wells also have been described which possibly were used for drinking and irrigating small plots.[223]

In Jain literary book, Brihatkalpa-bhashya fields or cultivable lands were cleared in two categories *setu* and *ketu:* Setu had been used for such cultivable lands which were irrigated by *Arhat* or *Rahat* while irrigation of *ketu* depended on rains.[224] Through Jain literature, it is clear that different systems of irrigation existed in various areas. Indus area, it depended on rivers in Lat country, it depended on rains in Dravida areas, it depended on tanks in Uttarapath, it depended on wells.[225] A literary source of later period where material sources of irrigation were absent by adopting artificial sources of irrigation and the productivity of land was considerably enhanced. Thus, in the literary soucrces of both past and the future, there are plenty of examples available which illustrate several irrigation facilities provided by the state.

Inscriptions of Gupta period also indicate the keen interest taken by the state to provide irrigation facilities. Through these inscription, it is clear that peasants used lakes, tanks, wells etc for the purpose of irrigation. Words like Vapi, Tadag and Dirghika have been used for tank. Probably these words have been used for small, big and very big tanks in Gangadharpur plate of Vishwa Varman. These words are available and have been used for different types of tanks.[226] In the Raipur grant of Sudevraj only two types of tanks Vapi and Tadag have been used.[227] Dharsen's Maliye[228] grant Palitana grant[229] only word used for tank is vapi. In stone inscription of Gangadharpur, there is mention of construction of well in the modern Jalalabad district of Malwa, which shows that wells were used during this period for irrigation.

Through above descriptions, it is clear that the contemporary and inscriptional evidences prove availability irrigational facilities during that period. According to the economic importance of irrigation and agriculture irrigation plans were protected by the state government and encouragement were provided for their development. There was provision of punishment for those who harmed it.

Through Brihatsamhita written by Varahmihir and Amarkosh written by Amarsingh, we got elaborate knowledge of various aspects of agricultural works. According to Vijay Kumar Thakur Brihatsamhita written by Varahmihir is very useful source for last decade of the fifth and first decade of 6th century AD.[230] In these books, on the basis of astrological bodies i.e., planets, stars, and constellation positions on agriculture these provide much useful information.[231] The process of production was under very heavy pressure during that period due to which agriculture was not going on well. In order to ward off the problems of agriculture Brihatsmahita has suggested a number of solutions.

The 255 Indian plants have been described in Brihatsmhita,[232] preparing land for planting them and these all have been described in detail. Use of shisham as manure has also been mentioned in this. Varahmihir has told that sesamum plants chopped into small pieces when mixed with soil make very good manure. He has also discussed methods of grafting and preparing separate plants. Trees that can be grafted are jackfruit, ashok, banana, lemon, pomegranate, grape, big sweet lemon, jasmine etc. For preparing graft branch of tree is chiselled by one-third and tied to another. Similarly, chiselled branch is covered by cow dung mixed with earth.[233] During the course of time, when roots develop, thus, it is separated and shifted to another place. Varahmihir has also written about appropriate time and season for grafting. Varahmihir has said that grafting of branches without leaf in winter season, grafting of big branches in rainy season should be done.[234] Even in present days such experiments are carried out. Brihatssamhita has described the utility of various types of soil and its suitability for different types of plants for example eugenia, manira big sweet lemon grapes, lemon, pomegranate, jackfruit etc. can be grown in wet soil.[235] For good fruition a definite distance between two plants is compulsory.

Varahmihir has mentioned diseases infecting the plants and their remedial measures.[236] He has said that first of all infected part of the plant should be separated or cleaned and Baku should be put over that and water and milk should be sprinkled over that. If any plant has lost its capacity to produce fruits by putting water and milk it will again start giving fruits. In order to increase yield, a peasant should sprinkle powdered goat dung powdered shisham seeds, one handful of wheat flour one tola of beef and one drum of water for seven days.

While describing the treatments of plants Varahmihir has written that seeds should be soaked in ghee for ten days and everyday it should be taken out by applying ghee on hand. Then it should be mixed with cow dung, thereafter, it should be broadcasted in soil now this helps seeds to grow. Rice, flour of black gram, powdered shisham seeds, wheat flour should also be sprinkled on them. In order to prepare seeds of kapil roots of eight types of trees should be boiled in milk, now it should be cooled then seeds should be soaked in them for hundred seconds and thereafter dried in the sun for thirty days. Thereafter, it should be broadcasted in well prepared soil.[237]

If any seed is soaked in the paste of Akola, hundred times or in oil and put in soil, thereafter it germinates very fast.

Fa-Hien[238] has described Indus-Gangetic plains of Gupta period. It's evident from this that in those days lands on northern India were fertile. From Ritusamhar[239] of Kalidas, it is clear that there was abundance of plants in those days. Kalidas provides an attractive description of charming trees which came to bloom in different months. In his description, ashoka, dhak, champak, kadamba, keshar ketak and several other trees are covered. All these trees grew in those days in damp polar region of India.

During Gupta period, it's not only agriculture but horticulture[240] also was highly popular. Kamasutra written by Vatsyayan provides description of various types of orchards and gardens. It is very clear from this that particularly northern area were highly fertile Amarkosh[241] also discusses about matters related to soil fertile, fallow, desert, salty, grass covered, muddy, sandy, and rain irrigated soil in this period were in order called urara, ooshar, macro, preheat pankila shaekarwati davebhatta repectively.

In post-Gupta period, physical condition of land was more or less the same as in Gupta period from *abhidhanaratnamala*, we know about the soil and agriculture regarding this other knowledge about these provided by Medhatithi, Parashar and early travellers from Arab, from their works. During this period, main occupation of the people was farming as there was a land in plenty. According to Huen[242] Tsang the lands of Magadha and Malwa were very fertile which provide enough yield land of Kachchha were salty and sandy where flowers and fruits grew rarely climate of whole country was hot airy and dusty.[243]

Whatever was the period, the economic life of the people has not remained untouched from geographical reasons and effects of the situations, and particularly agriculture of ancient India was affected heavily. The economic life of the people in India of post-Mauryan period was to a great extent influenced by the natural climate such as soil, garrison of mountain, river network, vegetation and seasons because of strong rang. India remained naturally a well-protected country. The mountain of great Himalayas in the north and sea in the east, west and south was protected by the Bay of Bengal (eastern sea), Arabian Sea, and Indian Ocean respectively. India's divisions into five great areas in Madhya Pradesh, Uttarapath, Prachya (Eastern India), Dakshinapath (Decean) or Uparant (Western India) was known to the people even in those days. River Ganges flowing from Himalayas was the biggest and the most important river which can be compared with the river of Egypt, it was very important in post-Mauryan period.

In deciding the economic life of the people, the role of climate was important and that is so even today. The chilly cold winds coming from the north were not allowed to enter internal parts of India by snow-covered mountain peaks regularly which has helped the growth of crops[244] in India along with traders and seafarers also used monsoon air to their full extent. Physical specialities, climate, types of soil, production and from other point of views there are unevenness in different areas.

According to ancient Greek writers rain occurred twice in a year once in summer and second time in winter regularly[245] along with this clouds hovered in the sky[246] without any seasonal reasons. Therefore, three types of rains have been discussed in Milind Panaho.[247] As per geographical areas, the quantity of rain varied. In the stone inscriptions of Hathigumpha[248] and Junagarh,[249] it is mentioned that Kalinga and western India faced hurricanes and it rained very heavily. Repeated discussion about drought and famine showed instability and uncertainty of rain in certain parts of the country.[250] Very heavy rain, hurricane,[251] lightning and thunder, earthquakes[252] and hail storm and incidents like these which affected public life and destroyed valuable crops despite these all in totality the situation was very much favourable. Generally, the climates for the most number of months in India were such that kept people physically and mentally active.

Due to summer and winter rains in India, there were two crop seasons in India, during summer with the start of rain agricultural activities used to being and as has been desirable by Greek historians,[253] paddy, maize etc were sown during this period. Second crop season used to began in winter season when according to classical writers' wheat, barley, pulses and other food crops were grown. Three types of farming are arising due to of lack of rain i.e., chanchu, shwetashthi, and shalakvrith have been described in Buddhist book Divyavadan.[254] In areas with irregular rainfall, in order to evolve the drastic affects of famine, artificial irrigation system was made. Yet, on account of this, there used to be huge loss of life on a large scale.[255]

In the sources of this period, there are several references of flood. Hathi Gumpha cave inscription mentions that king Kharawela[256] had to repair gatewalls, building and means of irrigation caused by storm, and hurricane and vey heavy rains in the very first year of his reign. Junagarh inscriptions of

Rudradaman also makes it clear that due to heavy rain and hurricane below Urjayat (Modern Girnar) hill rivers i.e., Survaarnsikate (modern Suvarna rekha), Palasini were flooded due to which banks of Sudarshan lake collapsed. The king got the repair works of the banks done strongly in order to reduce the agony of the subjects. Through these examples, it was known that flood was a common speciality of ancient Indian economy and the the farmers had to bore the burnt of it.

Though from the very ancient Indian time, scientists on the basis of observation of space predicted either scarcity or plenty of rain. These forecasts have been made on the basis of positions of different planets, direction of wind etc which were usually true.

It was believed during Gupta period that seeds sown in the beginning of particular constellation yielded good crops. These constellations were Do Dharti, Mool, Patra (most probably Magha), Pushya, Tin Hasta, Tin Uttra, Revate, Dhanishtha and Ashwini. Some scholars believe the word Fani used in this period as synonym of sun. But it is wrong because Narada has clearly expressed it as Rahu supporting which Kashyap says next light, constellations from Rahu are unfortunate.[257] To decide opportune moment for agriculture, Vashistha[258] says that three constellations of stars from the first from sun are not good time for ploughing the fields are rather unfortunate. Eight Nakshatras after that are fortunate, nine Nakshatras after that are unfortunate and eight after that are again fortunate ones. Examples, if Surya is combined with Ardra Nakshtra then the nakshtra before that will be Margasheersha. Beginning from this first three or Margasheersha Ardra and Hunarrashee will be unfortunate while Pushya, Ashlesha, Magha, Purva, Phelguni, Haste, Chitra and Swati will be fortunate Nakhatras. Vishkha Anuradha, Jyestha, Mool, Purvaasharh, Uttarasshharh, Abhijeet, Shravana and Dhanishtha Nakshtras will be unfortunate while Shatimisha, Purvabhadra, Uttarabhadra, Revati, Ashwini, Bharani, Kritika and Rohini will be fortunate ones.[259] Narad[260] also says that for begining of plouging one Nakshatra before sun to three Nakshatras are harmful for the bullocks. Three Nakshatras after this are wealth giving and give five other happiness as well. Nine Nakshatra after this provide three types of benefits while the next five give wealth and other three Nakshatras are fortunate.

Varahmihir in his work in Brihatsamhita on the basis of his studies of space has made forecast about sufficient rain, too much of rain, and lack of rain. He has described Manak Varsha.[266] Mapak (an equipment for measuring rain). Though existence and extent of India of Gupta period is not available (well-established), but various types of calamities, i.e., drought, too much of rain, tremors, plague, epidemics and man-made diseases spreading in animals have been described in Brihatsamhita of Varahamihir.[262]

Varahmihir has cited a number of instances of too much rain and over-flooding causing extensive damage of crops. Best example of such incident is Junagarh inscription of Samudra Gupta wherein it is recorded the damage caused to Sudarshan lake due to very heavy rain.[263] We get also the description of Vitasta and Mahapid lakes of Kashmir over-flooding which caused famine.[264] By piling up resources to word off such fearful agonies of the subjects was the responsibility of the state.

Varahmir has also done forecasts about earthquakes. Though there is no definite proof available about such tremors during Gupta period.[265] During famine in Gupta period steps are taken to provide benefit to the people is also lacking in direct evidence. However, direct evidences of drought and famine are available from Dharsan-II of Maliya copper plate inscriptions, Samudra Guptas Allahabad pillar inscription and Gwalior stone inscription. Thus, from ancient times itself, the geographical factors are also one of the reasons which affect on the country's agriculture in a serious manner.

References

1. Parmeshwarilal Gupta, Gupta Samrajya. Varanasi, 1970, page 450.
2. Ram Sharan Sharma, Prachin Bharat Me Rajnitik Vichar Ayam Sansthayin.
3. Radhakishna Chaudhay. Prachin Bharat ka Arthik Itihas.
4. Parmeshwari Lal Gupta, referred earlier, page 365.
5. Kamandak, Niti Shastra, 220
6. Raghuvansh, 16.2.
7. Narada Smriti, 11.23.
8. Vishnu Smriti, Julius Jouly, Chaukhambha Prakashan Varanasi, 1962, ii. 3.
9. Parmeshwari Lal Gupta, above referred, page 450.
10. Yagyavalkya Smriti. 1.166 Vrihatsamhita 16.3.
11. Manusmriti, 8.415.
12. Narad Smriti, 5.25 – 44.
13. Parmeshwarilal Gupta, above referred , page 450.
14. Shri Ram Goyal, Gupt Samrajya ka Itihas, Jodhpur 1995 Page 405.
15. Shukranit, 4.2.24, 2 -44.
16. Raghuvansh , 5,8,9.
17. S.K. Maity, Economic life of Northern India in the Gupta Period, page 96.
18. Kamandak, Nitisar, E.Vidyasagar , J.P, Calcutta, 2.20.
19. Vahi.
20. Raghuvansh, E Velankar, H.D. Bombay, 1948, 16.2.

21. Shukarnite – E. Sarakar . B.K. Allahabad, 1914, 1.311 Amarkosh,ii.
22. Narada Smirit T. Jauly, J. Oxfor, 1889,2.23.
23. The Tiprah Plate. Epigraphy India, 15 page 307.
24. Shukranite, 4.2.242-44.
25. Supada, page – 83-90.
26. Raghuvansh – 52.
27. Brihaspati Sriti -- Tr. Jauly, J. Oxford, 1889, 22,23-24.
28. Vahi, 22.25.
29. Brihaspati Smriti, - 23.5.
30. Brihaspati Smriti – 23.5.
31. Brihaspatismriti-23.5.
32. Naradsmriti, 14.4.
33. S. K. Maity., above referred page 99.
34. Narada Smrite, 29.
35. S. K Maily, above referred page 99.
36. Fleet, page 171.
37. Radhakrishna Chaudhary, above referred, page 101.
38. Radhakrishna Chaudhary, above referred, page 101..
39. Narada Smiriti.
40. S.K Maity above refereed page 9.
41. Brihaspati Smriti, 16.1 – 3, 9-14.
42. Indian History Quarterly – 4, 1930, page 53-56.
43. Narada Smriti, 6.3-5.
44. Brihaspati Smriti, 16.1 -3, 9-14.
45. Naradasmriti, 6.3.
46. Narada Smriti, 6.4.
47. Narada Smriti, 6.5.
48. Narada Smriti, 5.23.
49. Brihaspati Smrite, 15.9.

50. Brihaspati Smriti, 14.1.
51. Brihaspati Smriti, 16.1-2.
52. Brihaspati Smriti 16.3.
53. Brihaspati Smriti, 16.5.
54. S.K. Maity above referred, page -112.
55. Brihaspati Smriti, 13.27.
56. S. K. Maity, above referred, page -112.
57. Narada Smriti, 13.51.
58. A.L. Basham. Adbhut Bharat, Agra, 1988, page 192.
59. S.K. Maity, above refereed page 9.
60. Manu Smriti, 9-44
61. S.K. Maity, above referred, page -20.
62. Narada Smriti, 184.
63. Narada Smriti, 1-85.
64. Narad Smriti, 1-86.
65. Narad Smriti, 1-87.
66. Brihaspati Smirit, 7.27-28.
67. Brihaspati Smriti,- 7.44.
68. Brihaspati Smriti – 47.
69. Brihaspati Smriti 54.
70. Brihaspati Smriti 60.
71. Narada Smriti, 1.96.
72. Yugyavalkya Smriti, (Ed) Ganapati Shastri, Trivendrum, 1924, 2-28.
73. Brihaspati Smriti, 2.28.
74. Narad Smriti, 1.86.
75. S. K. Maity, above referred, page 18.
76. S. K. Maity, above referred, page 18.
77. D.N. Jha. The Revenue System in post-Mauryan and Gupta period , page 25.
78. Yagyavalkya Smriti, 2.24.
79. Yagyavalkya Smriti.

80. Yagyavalkya Smriti.
81. N.N. Kher: Agrarian and Fiscal Economy, in the Mauryan and post-Maurayan Age, Motilal Banarsidas, Delhi 15 ....1973.
82. S.K. Maity above referred, page 23.
83. Brihaspati Smriti, 16, page 119.
84. Fleet, page 52.
85. Yagyavalkya Smriti 1.337.
86. Vishnu Smriti, 3.67.
87. Yagyavalkya Smriti, 2.36.
88. P.N. Banerjee, Public Administration in Ancient India, page 72-73.
89. S.K. Maity, above referred page 26.
90. Fleet, page 263.
91. Fleet, page 127.
92. Abhigyan Shakantalam, 6 page 962-63.
93. Brihaspati Smriti, 16.119.
94. Brihaspati Smriti 18.58.
95. Narada Smriti, 13.51.
96. Manu Smriti,7, page 130-32.
97. Raghuvansham, 2.66,5.8.
98. Raghuvansham, 17.65.
99. Logge, page 42-43.
100. D. Damodarpur plate, D.C. Sarkar, 15, page 113.
101. Vishnu Smriti,iii,55.
102. Indian Antiquity, 1810, page 214.
103. Indian Antiquity, 1910, Page 214.
104. History of Dharmsastra, part 2, page 868.
105. N.N. Kher, referred earlier, page 42.
106. Campbell, Modern India, page 82.
107. H.S. Main, Village Communities in East and West, page 94.

108. Corpus Inscriptionum Indicarum, 3, Ed, page 170.
109. In Bengal 'Khasland' means State old land.
110. Ashutosh Mukherjee, Silver Jubilee Commemoration, Vol. III, part-2, page 486-87.
111. Same, page 487.
112. Coplife, page 186.
113. The Vakatak and Gupta age, page 333.
114. S.K. Maity, referred above, page -23.
115. Majumder, Corporate life in ancient India, page 186.
116. D.N. Jha, referred above, page 23.
117. Manusmriti, 8-262.
118. Yagyavalkya Smriti, 2, 154.
119. Narada Smriti, 11.2.
120. Brihaspati Smriti, 19.26.
121. Brihaspati Smriti, 19.33.
122. Hindu Polity, Page 343.
123. U.N. Ghoshal, referred above, page 58.
124. A.L. Basham, referred above, page 110.
125. Epigraphia Indica, 15.130.
126. Epigraphia Indica, 20.63.
127. Epigraphia Indica, 21.81-15.
128. Epigraphia Indica, 17.347-1.8.
129. Epigraphia Indica, 15.143-1.8.
130. Fleet, 16.166.
131. Varahmihir, Brihatsamhita, (Ed.) M.R. Bhatta, Delhi 1992, xv, 9,10, XXX111, 9.
132. Above mentioned.
133. Same XCVII.6; XCL4.
134. Same XXXIX.14.
135. Same XLV.621 LXVII.3.
136. Same XV.4,7,11,47.

137. Brihatsamhita, VIII.13.
138. Same V.21.27,78.90.
139. Same IX43, XXV.2.
140. Same VIII, 8,9,12.
141. S.K. Maity above referred, page 106-07.
142. Brihatsamhita, L III, 61.
143. Same, L III, 89.
144. Same V.39, VIII 30.
145. Same XXXIX. 2.
146. Same XXIX.3; L-30.
147. Same XXIX. 2.
148. Same L 30; LXX. 8.
149. Same XXIX. 2.
150. Same VII, 4.
151. Same XIV33; XL 5.
152. Same XV.6; XVI.7.
153. Same XXIX6; XL.4.
154. Same VIII 10; XXIX.4.
155. Same V.75; XV.14.
156. Same XV14; XVI 36; XXV.2.
157. Same XL.2.
158. Same XXIX.5; XV.14; XX1.3.
159. Same XXIX.5; XV.14; XVI.3.
160. Same V.75; XV.14.
161. Same XXIX.5; XL.5.
162. Same XLIII.5; XLVII,3.5.
163. V.75;XV 9.
164. XXXIX.6.
165. XXIX.6;XIX 6.
166. LIV.120.
167. Same LV10X11.

168. Amarkosh, 2.9; 3.9.
169. Raghuvansham, 1.50,4.20,37.
170. Amarkosh,3.9.
171. Indian History Congress Proceedings Volume, 1973.
172. Atharva Veda, 1.34.
173. Diodorus, 2.36.
174. Brihatsamhita, 2.36.
175. Amarkosh, 9.43.
176. Raghuvansham, 4.34.
177. Cosmos,9.44.
178. M.S Randhava, A History of Agriculture in India, Vol. 1, page 401.
179. Agriculture in Ancient India, I.C.A.R. (Ed.) D. Randhawa, 1964, page 34.42.
180. Amarkosh, 3.13-14.
181. Brihaspati Smriti, VIII, 79-80.
182. Cosmos. XI , page 358.
183. Shukraniti IV, 38-39.
184. Amarkosh, 9.13.
185. Agriculture in Ancient India.
186. Amarkosh, 9.13.
187. Same, 9.26.
188. Chullabagga , 8,1.2.
189. Sino – Indian Studies, 1946 page 43.
190. Diodorus Siculus, ii 36; Dionicus Perejires, ii 1085-1165.
191. Early History of North India Sudhakar Chattopadhyay, page -118
192. Ramayan Balkand, V, Ayodhyakand, 85 etc.
193. A.N. Kher, Agrarian and Fiscal Economy, In the Mauryan And Past Mauryan Period., page 105.

194. Brihatsamhita, A -58.
195. Agnipuran, A 281.
196. Nitisar, VI.7.
197. Agricutlure in Ancient India, I.C.A.R page 43.
198. Referred in Dharmakosh , Ed. Laxman Shashtra Joshi, 1937-41.
199. Manusmiriti, VIII.248.
200. Same IX 279.
201. Dharmkosh1, Part III (1609); 5.
202. Ancient India, (A-1), No. 11; page 16.
203. Indian antiquity a review, 1954-55, page 14.
204. Above refereed, page 7.
205. Above referred, page 19.
206. Above referred, page 16.
207. H.D. Sankaliya report on the excavations at Nasik and Jorwe, 2050-51.
208. R.S. Sharma, light on Early Indian Society and Economy.
209. F. Kilhorn, Mahakavya of Patanjali, 1.11.
210. Manusmriti, IX,274.
211. D.C. Sarkar Select Inscriptios page 119, line 1-8.
212. G.L. Adya, Early Indian Economics, page 40.
213. Shyam Sundar Nigam, Economic Organisation in Ancient India page -114.
214. Kamandak, IV 51 and 52.
215. Narada Smiti, XI, 18.
216. Same, XI. 20.
217. Same, XI. 21.
218. Brihaspati Smriti, XX 1115.
219. Amarkosh, 9.36, page 67.
220. Above referred 9.7 page 62.
221. Same, 9.28 page 66.

222. Malvikagnimitram, 11 page 1010.
223. Amarkosh, page 10, 62.
224. Brihatkalp kavya, 1.826.
225. Same. 1.1239.
226. Corpus Inscription un-Indicarum, VVI-III, page 75, line 22.
227. Same, page 199, line 25-26.
228. Same, page 166, line 25-26.
229. Same Epigraphia Indica, XI, plate 1, page 107, line 16, plate –II, page II, Line 18, plate III, page 113, Line - 16.
230. Vijay Kumar Thakur, Agrainan Scan in the Brihatsamhita proceedings of the Indian history congress, 59th season, 1998, page 38.
231. Vijay Kumar Thakur, Urban Decay, ecological imbalance and Brihatsamhita.
232. Same, LIV 120.
233. Same, LV 2.
234. Same, LV 4, 5.
235. Same, LV 10, 10.
236. Same, LV 14, 18.
237. Same, LV 19, 30.
238. Same, page 412.
239. Same, page 413.
240. Same, page 416.
241. Same, page.
242. Same, page 423.
243. Same, page 424.
244. Cortius Reform Quomtis , The history of Alexander the Great, Book.
245. Diodorus, II 36.5; Strabo, XV 1-13, XV.1-20.

246. Ad. Dharmasutra, 1.3; 11.31; Gautam Dharm, XVI 10; Milind Panaho, Trechner (ed), page 114, Manu IV, 104.
247. Second books of the East, 171 Milindpanho, page 114.
248. Epigraphia Indica, XX, 721; Indian Historical Quarterly Vol XIV, page 474.
249. Epigraphia Indica, VIII, page 42 ff; Selected Inscriptions 169 ff.
250. Mahavastu – 1,346, Milindpanho, page--8, Ramayana, 1,9.9.
251. Ad. Dharm Sutra, 1.3; II 8, Gautamdharm XVI. 5; Man IV 102.
252. S.N. Kher, referred above, page 101.
253. Diodorus, 11.36, Strabo; XVI 38.19.
254. Same.
255. Divyavadan, page 131.
256. Ramayan Kishkindhakand, 28; Mahavastu, III 303; Cortiyasee, VIII.IX.
257. Epigraphia India, XX, 72 F; Indian Historical Quarterly page 261 ff.
258. Agriculture in Ancient India, I.C.A.R , page 112.
259. Same.
260. Same.
261. Same.
262. Dr. R.K. Chaudhary, Economic History of Ancient India, issue – 1981, page – III.
263. S. K. Maity, Economic life in Northern India, page 113.
264. Rajatrangini , V 68-71; 80 etc.
265. S.K. Maity referred above, page 245.

2

Peasants Structure

Emergence of Intermediaries out of Land Grants

There are rare examples of land grants in the early period.[1] But in early *Dharma Sutras*[2] land grants have been described as a very pious donation washing out all sins. According to Manu,[3] a donor of land begets land only in lieu of it. One chapter of *Mahabharata* (praise of land donation) is exclusively dedicated to land grant.[4] Besides this in other literary sources, and land grant charters a number of statements are found related to it make it clear that donation of land in this period had become an institution.

Through sources we get information about several types of donees i.e., *Brahmins,* Buddhist Sanghas, royal officers class, members of royal family, such villages which supplied military to the king, temples and gods and helpless, hunters etc. The land- grant charters generally issued by king, queen, feudal lords, provincial rulers and other royal officers. Personal land-grant charters were mainly issued by guild organisations and common men (followers).

Various writers of *Smritis* have impelled rulers to donate lands to *Brahmins.*[5] According to *Arthashastra* (written by Kautilya), we come to know that the land to be given to *Brahmins* were given to such *Brahmins*,who performed *Yagyas* (Ritviks) or those who performed the job of *Purohit* and performed the job of spiritually guiding the people and other such *Brahmins,* who were scholars of Vedas.[6] Brahmins were even given forest land for the purpose of spiritual and religious studies, contemplation and penance.[7] Nasik and Karle Buddhist cave inscriptions of Usavada,[8] Mayidavelu (Guntur district) copper plate inscription in the last phase of Singh Varman[9] (anscestors of Shivaskand Varman) in the last phase of 3rd century, Shivaskanda Guptas.

Hirahadgalle copper inscription (1st quarter of 4th century[10]), Brihasflayan dynasty Jayavarman's Kondamdi[11] copper inscription (last phase of 3rd century) etc., are the inscriptional evidences of land being given to *Brahmanas.* Though there is no description of donees but by the nature of the donation it is clear that the land were given to *Brahmins.*

In Nanaghat cave inscription of queen Naganika[12] there is description of one village on the occasion of Ashwamedha Yagya (sacrifice) 1st BC. In this Vedic sacrifice the donee seems to be *Brahmin* only. Buddhist cave inscription of Nasik[13] of 2nd AD of the period of Nahapan mentions that Nahapans' son–in-law and son of Dinika Usavdatta defeated Malayajas and went to Pushkara Lake near Ajmer and he donated a village. According to S. Chattopadhyay donees were Indian Brahmin only because Pushkar in Ajmer area is a religious place of Hindu or *Brahmins.*[14] Just like this Ikshvaku inscriptions[15] found in Krishna of Guntur Andhra province makes it clear that king Shantamoola first performed a sacrifice and besides other presents donated land as well. Here both the donor and donee were *Brahmins.* Besides this Pali religious literature is full of examples of royal land donations given to *Brahmanas.*[16] *Brahmadeya* land grants were replete with exemptions and prerogatives. Accordig to Arthasastra the land donated to *Brahmanas* should be free from taxes and punishments (Adandakarani).[17] Proof of these is written donation letters. For example, it is said Madiyavelu inscription "donated Viripara village will be equipped with freedoms of Brahmdeva donations."[18]

Even at personal level lands were donated to *Brahmins. Brahmin* religious books seem to encourage such donations. But at personal level, donor had to face some problems in getting such lands freed from taxes. Therefore, donor had to seek prior permission from the state on payment of some amount towards compensation for revenue losses. Some *Brahmins* became rich by accepting land donations from state and individuals. Getting donated land was their main source of livelihood. Produce from such lands were used on the occasions of religious functions and their organisations.[19]

Most donations given by Satavahanas and Shaka rulers to the Buddhist Sanghas were for the purpose of the welfare of Buddhist religion. Therefore, Buddhist community was equipped with special rights within their rule. Purpose behind such donations was to earn piousness by the donor.

Two Nasik Buddhist cave inscriptions of Gautamiputra Satkarni[20] (117 AD and 130 AD Karle Buddhist cave inscription 130 AD) two other of Pulumawi Nasik Bauddhist cave inscription,[21] (142 AD to 145 AD of Pulumawi)[22] and Nahapan's son-in-law, Usavdattas Nasik and Karle Buddhist cave inscriptions[23] (2nd AD) are the evidences of lands grants provided for the livelihood of various seats of Buddhism. Besides these, Buddhist literature is also full of several texts of land being donated to Bauddhists and their disciples.[24]

The freedoms and exemptions given on lands donated to Bauddhist Sanghas are almost alike in all inscriptions. Thus, neither royal army could enter nor government officials could interfere and district police could intervene or hinder in any manner in distributed landscape.[25]

Archaeological and literary sources are full of examples of land grants to Buddhist monks on personal level. Even to the extent that a woman, a prostitute, a girl, and eunuch and a robber has also donated land.[26] Buddhist literature is replete with evidences as land grants on individual level. As for example Jetawan Aram[27] (garden) in Shravasti was donated by a trader Anathpindak (Sudant), a garden in Rajagrih by royal physician Jetwan Aram[28] (garden) by a man named Goshringi, mango orchard[29] by royal donor Amrapali[30] and a big forest[31] were donated by the republic of Lichchavi etc. Thus, the private donations made for the welfare of Buddhist Sanghas were religious and spiritual in nature. Officers of the state were granted land donations in lieu of their service rendered to the state by them.

Kautilya says that a *Dhyakshas* of different departments, Accountant, Gopas, army men, veterinary doctors (*Anikathas),* physicians, trainers, of horses (*Ashwa Dammaka*) and ambassadors should be given land.[32] Like this spies working within the kingdom should also be given land.[33] Senapati Gram stated in Mahavastu seems to be royal donation received in lieu of their services.[34] In Manusmriti[35] and *Mahabharata*[36] it is mentioned that officers dealing with 10, 20 and 100 villages should be donated land for their livelihood. Even in Jataka books land donation for officers' appointed by the state in its services is mentioned.[37] These land donations look like *Jagirs* and there was a ban on selling purchasing and mortgaging such lands (Vikayadhanabragam).[38]

Even members of the royal family were given land donations for their livelihood. In *Arthashastra,* there is mention of land donated by queen and princes.[39] Besides some inscription there is mention of such donations even in *Ramayana*[40] and Jataka[41] books. Thus, the system of donating lands to the members of royal family was commonly in practice.

In *Arthashastra* there is also mention of different kind of land donation which was based on armed services. In these lands of particular village was left under their control for providing (*Ayudhya*) supply of army.[42]

Land was also donated to temples and institutions of this type. Nasik and Karle Buddhist cave inscription of 2nd century AD of Usavadatta makes it clear that some villages were donated.[43] It is clear from Mallawalli of Vishnukadda, Chutu Satakarni of 3rd century AD that one village was donated to God Malapal.[44] Through one inscription of Shri Vijay Skand Burman, a Pallava ruler of the last quarter of the 4th century, it is clear that *Baghwan Narayan* temple located at Dalura was donated on area.[45] At personal level also people donated lands to temple.

Atithya word described in *Arthashastra* bas been described by its interpreter, commentator Bhattaswamin as such lands has been donated to officers for the welfare of the people or for carrying out religious works.[46] This was like *Inam* (reward) and *Muafi* of the Mughal period which was similar to lands donated to *Brahmins* and Buddhist Sanghas free of all taxes and equipped with special powers.

Land was donated for royal support also. Therefore, there is description of barbers,[47] hunters,[48] disabled, helpless[49] and traders[50] as donees. In Manusmriti, there is description of pupil donating land along with so many other gifts.[51] In Buddhist cave inscription of Nasik there is mention of Dhambika village which was donated by the villagers.[52] It is not clear whether city corporation had any right to receive any donation of land or not but in any such condition, prior approval of the king was necessary. Sometimes in the process of donation of land, double transfer of land used to take place. In such a case, the land was purchased, first by the donor and this was donated to the done. Subsequently, it is mentioned in Buddhist cave inscription of Usavdatta that he purchased a land from a *Brahmin* named Ashwabhuti in 4000 Karshapan[53] before donating the same to Buddhist Sangh, Jetwan Aram (garden) in Shravasti was purchased by Anathpindak before he donated that the Buddhist *Matha.*[54]

Rights related to land donation of woman had been accepted by this time. In a pillar inscription of Ashoka, it is described that his second wife is mother of Tiwar, Karuvaki had donated a mango orchard.[55] Gunapady was issued by Charudevi, the queen of young king Shrivijay Budhburam can in the period of Shrivijay Skand Berman in the 1st quarter 4th centruy[56] AD. Even in Buddhist literature, there are references of women donating land.[57] But during Gupta period Narada[58] finalised a law that lands transferred by woman particularly donation and sale should be treated unlawful.

Donated lands used to be of different types, i.e., fertile, fellow, forest land, orchard etc. But lands used for donation used to be fertile, which may sustain the burdens of the donee. In one of the inscription[59] of Satvahana period, there is a description that if the land be uncultivable, villagers of that village did not live there. Though there used to be every type of land in donated villages. Forests and orchards were donated to Sanyasis hermits and Buddhist temples, so that they may conduct their activities uninterrupted. Probably, along with changes in dynasties or kings donations were renewed. Mallavalli pillar inscription[60] of king Shivaskanda Buman (first quarter of 4th century) refers renewal of a donated village.

According to Fleet[61], in a situation of the change of a dynasty, donated lands were vigorously verified, prior to their renewal evidences of such renewals are available in plenty in other inscriptions in case one is not the owner of a particular land, he can not donate the same without being owner of that land. If donation is made such donations will fail and will be unfructuous.[62] In order to stop irregularity of any kind, illegal donations were kept protected under a responsible officer. Manu[63] also propounds this law in donation should be declared illegal. Thus, all personal donations were minutely scrutinised before being actually taken advantage thereof by the donees.

Officers were intimated to the announcement of royal donations in order to avoid any interference on their part. In the Hirahadgalli[64] copper plate inscription, King Shivaskand Burman, a long list of state officers is given who were intimated about donations.

Originally, authorisation letter of donation was woven on a thick cloth or inscribed on a copper plate but due to problems in protecting them these were inscribed on the walls of caves or on pillars. We get information from the *Vaishnav Dharmasastras* that at the time of grants, the king should provide a document inscribed either on cloth or on copper plate to the donee on which the name of donor and his three ancestors area of the donated land, prohibitive order against the violators should be mentioned and seal of royal officers are stamped.[65] It seems this letter used to be prepared by high officials i.e., ministers,[66] privy council (for *Rahasyadhikrita*)[67] and army chiefs (Mahadandanayaka).[68]

Generally, the ruling class after issuing the royal donations send the decree to the district level officially to complete other essential formalities. Nasik and Karle Buddhist cave inscriptions of Gautami Satkarni,[69] Nasik Buddhist cave inscription of Vashisthputra Shripulumavi,[70] copper plate inscription of Hirahadagalli of Shivaskanda Burman[71] etc., are its examples. But land donations were even given by feudal lords. For example, son-in-law of Nahapan, and provincial governor Usavdutta issued three land grant charters,[72] Maharathi Somdas feudal lord of king Pulumavi issued royal donation of a village.[73]

State donation of 100 villages is the example of the highest donation given,[74] referred in these sources. Eighty villages donated by king Chulani has been described in Mahamagga Jatak.[75] There is repeated description of donated villages.[76] Thus, through the study of these descriptions of it is clear that there was no constitutional limit on generosity shown or pity taken by a king.

The letter of order issued by the king for compliance of authorisation letter, registration and arrangement of registration of donation to be given to donee was done. In donation specially freedoms were mentioned and particular care was taken for mentioning this.[77] Thus, land grant related every record was preserved by the state. On the basis of this analysis, it can be said that during this period a large number of donees were created, who were equipped with special powers. Because land donations were equipped with certain freedoms this harmed the state coffer and along with this the grip of the state also loosened on the donated land.

In Gupta period, most of the lands were donated to either *Brahmins* or Buddhist or Jain Sanghas. Mostly king, queen, state officials, individuals and guilds were the donors whose aim was to earn piousness. In this period, we get such an example of land donation also where in a *Brahmin* had donated land to another *Brahmin*. This *Brahmin* was Vasudeoswamin of Barakamandal, who donated a piece of his land to a religious *Brahmin* named Somaswamin for earning piousness for himself and his ancestors.[78] perhaps Vasudeoswamin was such a *Brahmin,* who had no knowledge of Vedas.

There are some such situations also where in the land was first purchased and they were donated to religious organisations. In the Damodarpur, copper plate inscription of Buddha Gupta's reign, it is mentioned that some habitable land was purchased to donate the *Brahmins.*[79] The adoption of this process has also been mentioned in three copper plate inscriptions recovered from East Bengal of Dharmaditya and Gopichandra's period.[80] In this period, some such evidences are also found which mentions some high officials requesting king to donate land to religious institutions. Example, Gunaigarh inscription makes it clear that on the request of king Rudradatha Vinay Gupta donated lands to Sanghas related with Mahayana sect.[81]

In several situations, the king himself from religious point of view gave land as donation. Proofs of such royal donations are copper plate inscriptions of Nalanda and Gaya of Samundra Gupta,[82] Bihar stone pillar inscription of Skanda Gupta,[83] Bhitari pillar inscription of Skanda Gupta,[84] sometimes from religious point of views queens also donated land.[85] From the same point of view, feudal lords of Gupta period also donated land.[86] Some officers of the state also did this job, for example. Officer Amararka Deo of the period of Chandragupta 2nd donated some lands of Ishwarovasak village to Arya Sangha of Karandabota (Sangh).[87] From religious point of views at personal level also some persons donated land,[88] just like this, even the inscriptions of later period; it becomes clear that the donors of above mentioned situations continued to donate land.

Land donations were made under some procedures one particular decorum were adopted. Vakataka queen Prabtrawat, Gupta's Ridhannpur[89] plate and Khoh plate inscriptions of Maharaja Sarvanth[90] makes it clear that the intimation of declaration of donations was given to village chief, *Brahmanas,* respected families elders *(kutumbins)* state officials and others.

The motive behind this was to give guarantee that no injustice has been committed during the donation of land.[91] In this act, approval of officials and village elders were therefore, necessary because first of all they investigated the prayer of donor and further referred it to local *Lekhadhikari* for further investigation. Finally like Hindu donation ceremony was ended by offering water.[92]

Sometimes land was donated by the donor for the fulfilment of some particular objective and sometimes for pious gains.[93] Chammak copper[94] plate inscription and Maharaja Pravarsen-IInd, Sivani[95] copper plate inscription makes it amply clear that donations made by the king-oriented towards earning virtue, power, victory and expansion of state.[96] The purpose of giving donations was to bear the expenses of worship of gods and goddesses. Besides these, donations were given for incurring the expenditure of this sacrifices (a flower, sandal etc.), rice (rice and other grains which were boiled in milk and mixed with butter and ghee, shatre (*Dharmashalas*), scent, incenses, garlands, wicks and repair of the temples. As it is clear from the Sanchi stone inscription of Chandragupta-IInd, for the food of Buddhist monks and lighting the wicks, land used to be donated permanently.[97]

In land grants revenue related exemptions, other immunised were specifically mentioned. Such common conditions have been repeated in the inscription of the Gupta and the post-Gupta period. Chammaka copper plate inscription of Maharaja Pravarsen[98]-II mentions that land grants were made to 1000 Brahmans. It also mentions the conditions and procedures of the land grants. In this inscription of Gupta period, for the first time, we hear the words of caution for the donee that he should work only in the interest of the villagers and the state. Though the taxes from which the donee was exempted and the special powers that were transferred to him were mentioned in detail. Along with this, the villagers were told to pay fees and state taxes and obey his orders. This fact can be seen mentioned in the Khoh land grant inscription of Sarvanath.[99]

Narada and Brihaspati have mentioned and fixed some laws in this context. According to this only that much could be given towards donation without which also the head of the family could run his family smoothly. Such donations due to which family had to face difficulties did not add virtue rather it was condemnable.[100] The property earned by an individual could be donated by himself according to his will, but the properties gained in marriage or interested from ancestors were not approved to be donated.[101] Moreover with the concurrence of wife, other relatives, ruler, the property obtained in marriage, inheritance or from his valour got legal validity for donation.[102]

These writers of *Smiriti* books have also discussed such donations which were not legally valid. In case of donations were made out of fear, anger, hatred, sorrow or towards bribes, as a fun or cheating or fraud or given by a child, a fool or a person who is not the owner or under intoxication or madness or wrongfully given, by given to a scum, the donation was treated illegal.[103] Brihaspati says further that donation given under such conditions could be taken back by the donor.[104] But Narada goes one step further he states that donor who out of greed accepts such donations and donor who commits illegal donations, what he should not have given both are entitled to punishments.[105]

If we study the inscriptions of Gupta period minutely we come to this conclusion that a large chunk of land either was personally donated to *Purohits* or religious institutions. Copper plates and inscriptions available today of those days are just small fragments of the entire donations. In most of the case, donated land was free from revenues which affected the state coffers adversely.

In ancient Indian history, the period between 200-600 AD was the beginning of land donation which reached at peak at the end. This tendency to donate land to an extent brought an intermediary class between peasants and the rulers in this period which initiated the process of feudalisation of land and the emergence of local units of production. In the eastern part of modern Madhya Pradesh and northern and eastern Bengal, *Brahmins* and temples were donated cultivable lands. But there were some basic differences in land donation of Madhya Pradesh and land donations of Bengal. Whereas the land donations of Bengal were a result of sale and purchase of lands and thereafter these lands were transferred in Madhya Pradesh donations were issued by feudal lords, *jagirdars* and they gave entire village in donations.[106] Donations in Bengal were issued by the approval of officers of the Central government which were only free from taxes while in the land donations of Madhya Pradesh, besides freedom from taxes, some other administrative exemptions were also included. During the period of Pravarsen Vakatak king (5th century AD) and rulers related to him had begun to lose control over all sources of revenue. These sources included grazing fields and coal, production of salt (Black salt mines), and all treasures and investments.[107] State ownership of mines was an important feature of sovereignty.[108] Gradually, this also began to be handed over to the *Brahmins.* In several land donations of fourth and fifth century *Brahmins* were allowed to use the hidden wealth of the village.[109] One more important thing was that the donor did not retain the right to rule the inhabitants of donated villages. In Madhya Pradesh, we get some very clear examples of some bit villages donated to *Brahmins* by big feudal lords. Rulers of these villages clearly instructed the inhabitants, peasants and artisans to play not only current taxes to the donees but also to obey their orders.[110] Yet inscribed letters of power (Charters) of 5th century AD reveal the power to punish the thieves and robbers were retained by the ruler himself.

The number of land donations made by feudal lords is more than the number of land donations made by the rulers in the Central India whereas the question of quantum of donations is concerned stone inscription of Bihar (489 AD) of Skanda Gupta makes it after that the Gupta king donated entire village and almost on the same condition on which their feudal lords did it. By the above example, it is clear that this village was transferred as *Agrahara* in accordance with '*Akshay Nivi* (land tenurial nights). Gupta kings accorded clear sanction to these *Akshay Nivi* donations given on personal level in north and east Bengal and eastern Bihar. Sale and purchase of several types of fields were included in these donations. Transactions of this type were brought to practice only after being sanctioned by local officers of local bodies and the Central government. In such land donations which were given to *Brahmins* and temples, king used to get ready to forgo his share of production. It was believed that one-sixth of religious benefit virtues will be borne the state automatically in such private grants.[111]

Due to the social and political need and its pressure also resulted in several donations of land in Madhya Pradesh and other places. It is clear from the directions of *Kaliyug* that due to social upheavals, tax collection on regular basis and their distribution among *purohits* and other people had become very difficult. Therefore, *purohits* were provided and officers, king could not enter in these fields. This was their direct responsibility to collect taxes from the peasants and thus earn their livelihood themselves. Generally, land was donated to *Branmins* in exchange of their support for the royal power but from amongst them, sometimes may turn out to be incapable and dissolve. Therefore, in Pravarasena-II is grant, it has been mentioned in very clear words that one thousand

Brahmins, who have been provided village as donation should not betray him, should not kill *Brahmin*, should keep away from theft and immorality, should not try to poison the king, should not declare war against the king and should not cause any harm to any other village.[112] Very clearly, here, like the purpose of donation is not to secure their support but to stop them from opposing or going opposition. Donors i.e., kings feudal lords, and at personal level individuals. Whatever be their purpose, these donations helped emergence of such a powerful class which had powerful grip on the economic and political power. Because the number of land intermediary *Brahmins* kept on increasing and some of them left the profession of *purohit* and engaged themselves in the management of land and other worldly activities more and more.

Law establishment by Manu that revenue officials should be given land as donation towards their wages is also supported by the *Shantiparva* of *Mahabharata* and *Dharmshastra* of Gupta period but it is not supported to a certain extent by Chinese traveller Fa-Hien one excerpt but translation of this portion is doubtful according to this, all the kings servants, guards, servants all get emoluments but in every context emolument word cannot be taken for land donation.

Some scholars have expressed their view that in Bengal and in other parts of India the prevalent practice of land donation was not only confined to cultivable land and rural villages. Some parts of land of northern and eastern Bengal and some villages of Madhya Pradesh it may be true but in Gangetic basin, Gujarat and Maharashtra generally settled and cultivatable lands alone were given as land donations in several cases the lands given to *purohit* were notified to the *Brahmins* and other villages and cultivable lands alone were given as land donations. In several cases, the lands given to *purohits* were notified to the *Brahmins* and other villagers.

That indicates that *Brahmins* were not admitted to the villages as leading farmers. Yet again village and farming areas were given with *udrang* and families which included all kinds of liabilities. Along with that they were also free from all kinds of gifts, free labour, special powers and soldiers and constables were also not allowed to enter in them. This fact indicates that these were inhabited earlier. In most land donations of this period *aprahat, khil, bhumich-hidrabnyay* and *awanirbandhranyay* words used in their traditional sense only.

Due to land donation in some parts of the country, fragmentation of lands began. In northern Bengal even one and half *Kulyawapa* land also had to be purchased at four different places in small pieces[113] of land, the reason for this may be that the pieces did not want to be separated from their lands, but from this, we get an indication that there was scarcity of land and weight of population was growing on them day to day. Whatever be the measurement of *Kulyawap* but in this period we do not get to hear of Buddha periods 500 to 1000 acres farms or huge state farms of Maurya period. In inscription of *Kalchuri-Chedi* period chunks described do not indicate big piece of land. *Maitrak* rulers of Vallabhi in Gujarat also donated lands but even in this context same things can be said.[114] Though at times even four Kulyawapa land was available for sale but land was donated in fragments. Due to this, not only the size of the field was getting reduced but new fields of smaller sizes were being made. This process of partition encouraged fragmentation of land. There is no mention of fragmentation of landed property in early rules on inheritance in the Manu *Smriti* and the Yagyavalkya *Smriti*. First of all this has been mentioned on Narada,[115] Brihaspati[116] Samhita. Thus, during the middle and last phase of Gupta period huge joint peasant families who had huge chunks of lands started breaking into smaller units. In the fertile river, valley of northern India density of population was on an increase, therefore, no sooner than later, the division of land was approved, the fragmentation of land was accelerated.

Because *Brahmins* owned several plots of land, therefore, they were unable to cultivate them all, though according to some *Smritis* of those days they could adopt agriculture and doing so was fully justified. Conditions of transfer of lands in several contexts, *Brahmins* were not cultivating the land by themselves, short-term peasants cultivated them charter of fourth to sixth century of Maharashtra and Gujarat, there is clear arrangement of rights given to donee that he should use the land himself, allow others to use them cultivate them or allow others to cultivate on lease.[117] It is possible that some *purohits* might be cultivating themselves but this is decided that temples and *mathas* got them cultivated through others. According to Fa-Hien peasant and oxen were provided *vihars* and *mathas* along with fields and orchards for cultivation.[118] Contemporary inscriptions provide information that donees in certain cases replaced new peasants from old peasants and thus could remove their tenants.[119] Thus, due to religious donations *purohits* and temples could permanently or temporarily realise taxes from their peasants, but they kept this entire amount for their livelihood. No part of that amount was deposited as revenue in the treasury of the state. Outside the *mathas* and *viharas* one-sixth of the produce was deposited by the land owners in the state treasury but many of them got it cultivated by others. It seems that till this time number of independent and permanent farmers was getting reduced who could cultivate themselves and directly deposited the revenue to the government Fa-Hien is of the opinion that only those plough the fields of the king they pay the revenue and they are free to go and live wherever they wished.[120] This provides a hint that a large number of such peasants, who did not pay revenue to the state but, did so to the religious intermediaries. Kautilya has directed that in new villages the lands made cultivable that should be given to the peasants by the king.[121] But Yagyavalkya has given this ruling that land should be given to the peasants through landlords (owners of the land) not by the king (Mahispati), though in the absence of land owner, king himself was the rightful owner of roots, esculent tuber roots and fruits produced.[122] In organisation of lands Yagyavalkya provides three tiers, *mahipati* (king), owner of the land (landlord) and cultivators (peasants).[123] On an average Brihaspati has also supported the same. A *Smriti* writer of later period has made of clear that land owner comes as middle step i.e., in between the king and the man who ploughs the field.[124] These owners or landlords gave lands on lease to temporary peasants and if they show carelessness in cultivating, they could be punished.[125] Thus they lived on the revenues collected from these peasants. We do not have any means to decide that these intermediaries (landlords) were owners of the fields to what extent. But their number was so large that they prepared the economic base for the rise of feudalism.

This is natural that king himself being the biggest landlord, could donate land to the Brahmins and other beneficiaries without any difficulty. Therefore, due to this system, a new class of landlords emerged who had ownership right over landed property. They had such rights never before. Thus, we see the emergence of a class which possessed feudal property and also possessed feudal right together. Such landlords are never seen before at any stage of ancient Indian history. During the times of Buddha, we hear about some gently landlords but they were cultivating their lands (farms) through their slaves or peasant labour. It seems that state farms of Maurayans were also managed in the same way. During Pre-Mauryan and Mauryan period, we find some *Brahmins* who used the revenues of villages. Issuance of land charters during

Gupta and post-Gupta period was prevalent. A big landlord class emerged who were not only entitled to realise the land revenue but also got the right to enforce law and order. For example officers of the king could not enter the lands which were donated to *Brahmin* beneficiaries. Along with that they could decide the cases against beneficiary families and their properties. Thus, the religious section of the beneficiary class became very powerful on account of their control over not only spiritual thought but also fiscal economic and administrative powers.

Land donation had another consequences also, the decline of powers of peasants on land along with the loss of powers of the community on forests, grazing fields tanks etc. In the tribal and other autochthonous areas, in both of these conditions, peasants were reduced to slaves. In areas where number of labourers or population engaged in production was less, these communities were transferred to the beneficiaries and were told to live in donated villages and obey their new masters. They also fall prey to works without wages; but the occasions of such works without wages seldom arose and these were only limited to only carrying food materials military works and construction to roads. Due to this condition of peasants deteriorated. As these beneficiaries used to be present right on the spot their exploitation began in much more effective way. Thus, they achieved unauthorised intervention in various community sources, such as tanks, rivers, grazing fields, pasture land, forests, trees and plants.

During the course of time, the feudal relations that were developing in Indian situations had some specialities of its own. In India, small pieces of lands of peasants when compared with big chunks of lands were not connected from legal or economic point of views. In early medieval India, feudal landlords did not take any interest in organising farming on big chunks of land. For this purpose, peasants were not engaged in regular service of landlords. For the purpose of war or construction seldom such services were required. In India, agricultural slavery was never present as a common element but we see one type of slave, peasant class on whom intermediary landowners dumped the burdens of several types of taxes and liabilities. The type of free peasants i.e., free of all taxes, we find during the period of Buddha or Mauryas, there was severe decline in that in this period.

To substantiate theee prevalence of Indian feudalism the examples of the lack of the huge farms and *Jagirs* of the landlords and the prevalence of small scale peasants production can be put forward. What a peasant should grow on his land to the extent, it was decided by his professional needs and to the same extent on the demand of taxes by the beneficiaries. Beneficiaries on the force of charters issued in their favours used to demand all types of taxes from the peasants. But since land, bullocks and other agricultural implements were within the real powers of peasants, therefore in-between neo-landlords and established peasants clashes' and pushes and pulls were pertinent between them. But taken all together religious and ideological propaganda, peasant discontent was used to get pacified. Despite this if the peasants felt that situation has become intolerable they used to shift any area which was fallow land they could settle there and establish villages and could add to the units of production.

Perhaps larger part of the land remained under the control of such free peasants who paid taxes directly to the king. Due to increase in donated land during this period state treasury suffered a losing order, to compensate the losses therefore, besides paying a certain part to the state or regular tax; various other types of taxes were also imposed on the peasants. These all caused undoubtedly, further decline in the conditions of the peasants.

Ancient Indian states had complete knowledge of revenue system which was earlier a contribution to be made voluntarily[126] was made compulsory[127] in the later period. During Vedic period subjects and defeated enemies used to provide this (Bali).[128] In the later Vedic period, first of all we find the concept of taxes levied by the state on agriculture produce etc., to pay them was compulsory. Though there was no fixed rate seen in this period. There was one more tax in practice by the name of Shulka[129] in Vedic age, but nothing is known regarding its shape definitely. But till states were in their initial stage we are unable to know very much about taxes. During Mauryan period first of all revenue was fixed and regarding process of collection procedure profound law was framed. Along with rampant land donation to keep the treasury of the state wealthy and stable, during the 200 - 600 AD, amongst the people or subjects the number of taxes applicable there was further increase. This knowledge is available from *Smriti* books, epics, Buddhist literature and some inscriptions.

In ancient India, land revenue was the most stable source of wealth collection for the state. During Gupta period, the tradition of land revenue was affected because of large scale donation granted to the *Brahmin* donees.[130] In the opinion of Katyayan, king is entitled to revenue because he is the owner of land.[131] By this principle, the principle of revenue was tied to the feudal form. This provided the king legal right to donate land, but right of the land was restricted in this regard as while donating land he had to consult with the feudal lords. And he had to intimate about the donation given to those who's none of the interest or otherwise was involved in the land. By this procedure, in Indian revenue system tier-after-tier several layered revenue collection of feudal process began.

The architects of revenue system of Gupta period believed taxes given to the king as redemption in return of the protection provided to the subjects by him.[132] According to Adam Smith, the father of modern economics, every citizen should pay taxes proportionate to what he earns due to such protections that he gets from the state. According to Nitisar of Kamandka, the king should adopt the policy of a Gwala who first serves the cow and then milks it should not impose so much of taxes that the subjects' power to produce itself is destroyed.[133] But he has every right to exploit his bribe taking tyrannical officers.[134] According to Kalidas, taxes were imposed in the interest of the subjects. It is the duty of the king to use the wealth collected through taxes in such a way that the subjects get thousand times more benefits, as the sun sucks water from the sea and returns it back during rains many times more.[135] The voice of this principle of Kamandak and Kalidas reverberates in the views of Adam Smith and Stuart Mill.[136]

In the copper plate inscriptions of Gaya and Nalanda, Samudra Gupta had given Brahmins the powers to collect *uparikar* besides normal taxes from the villages. Its payees were family holders, artisans were kept out of its ambit of donors from others,[137] extra taxes were collected. Permanent residents paid taxes and temporary residents paid *uparikar* in several inscriptions there is mention of *uparikar.*[138] In the views of R.R. Dikshitar those people were collecting nominal taxes.[139] There is a mention in Raghuvansh that was imposed in the interest of the subjects.[140] From inscriptions, we get the information of following names of main sources of income, regular tax, periodical taxes, economic punishment, income out of the property of the state and presents received from the feudal lords.[141]

Two main types of land revenues are mentioned which were known as *udrang* and *uparikar*. This was a regular tax. But what part of his produce a peasant had to pay is not clear. Probably, wealthy paid in gold i.e., in cash form which was called *Hiranya.*[142] *Hiranya* was that form of agricultural production tax which was received in the form of Draya.

Dhanya was agriculture tax paid in the form of grains. Ghosal believes *Hiranya*[143] to have been fixed on the measure of land ploughed. Land tax used to be 1/6th of the produce as is known from the copper plate inscriptions of Faridpur.[144] This tax was collected on the basis of produce and not on *saurngs.*[145]

The number of land taxes kept on increasing while the number of trade taxes kept on decreasing. Probably 1-4th to 1/6th part was realised as taxes. Besides, whenever royal army passed through the villages it was the responsibility of local subjects to keep them safe. The state officials working in the rural areas for their livelihood took animals, grain, cots and other materials. In Central and Western Indian Royal army and officials used labourers without paying wages for their services which was called *Vishti* and it has been mentioned by Manu.[146] Digging wells in the villages, constructing roads in the country also *Vishti* forced taxes were taken. Its amount used to be fixed. Taxes were imposed on animals even. In Chammak copper plate inscription, imposition of taxes on cow, bullock is found mentioned.[147] *Bhutovat pratyay* was such a tax which was probably imposed on intoxicants grown inside the country or brought from outside.[148] *Shulk* or *chunge* was also collected as their fee was a traders tax. Its amount varied from articles to articles. If any trader was found trading without paying *shulk,* he had to pay eight times the amount as fine where the mention of *Klipt* and *Aklipt* taxes are also available.[149]

According to Fa-Hien, peasants paid a part of the produce as tax.[150] In course of time, number of tax payers kept on declining. According to what Fa-hien says "land revenues was paid by only those who ploughed the fields of the king.[151] State imposed taxes on free peasants and maintained his supremacy. Local officer gradually started grabbing economic power and began milking various advantages of various types which included extracting work without paying anything.

Shadbhag meant one-sixth which used to be the share of the king in the form of commodities. In Smriti etc., books kings share has been called *'Bali'* and not *'Bhag'*. According to Kautilya and Kalidas, Sanyasis also had to pay one-sixth of their savings.[152] The types of land and crop created difference in land revenue. According to Junagarh stone inscription of Rudradaman *'Bhag'*, 'Bali' and *'shulk* are terms for regular taxes.[153]

Kamandak has described eight sources of income of the state: Agriculture, transit routes, fort, bridge, elephant catching mines, building, woods, and colonising vacant places. Elephants and forts inclusion have been enumerated in this list because this instilled confidence among the traders due to which they could trade more and more and enriched the state.[154] Main source of the income of state were various land taxes, share in that was most prominent. Manu has decided its quantum probably on the basis of fertility of land, 1/th, 1/8th or 1/12th.[155] Writers like Kalidas and Narada[157] mention 1/5th and *Shukra*[158] of post-Gupta period mentions 1/6th, 1/3th, 1/4th or 1/2th in accordance with irrigation facilities as state share. Share has not been mentioned in the inscription of Gupta period, but in donation of Begram and Paharpur 1/6th share received by the king from land donations is of course mentioned. At least up to Gupta period, this tax was realised in the form of grains. In Arthasastra *'Bhag'* word has been used with some other taxes to indicate kings share in them such as *Udak Bhag, Lawan Bhag* etc. In Gupta inscriptions probably *Bhag* word along with *Bhag* and *Kar* is often seem as *'Bhagbhogkar'* or *Bhogbhagkar'*. Word *'Bhag'* is the name of *Bhog* in Manusmriti. D.C. Sarkar has accepted it as gift of flowers and fruits, plants, grass, woods etc., materials which were contemporary presents as gifts.[159]

'Kar' was common word for taxes and was also the name of a particular tax. In the Junagarh inscription of Rudradaman, *Visti, Begar* and *Pranay* have been accepted as emergency taxes.[160] In occasional taxes, *'Chatbhat Prawesh Dand'* has been mentioned. *Chatbhat* means police. When king or some important officers of the state were on their royal entourage, police and others also joined them. In order to meet these expenses, these taxes were collected from the people there.[161] Just like this, during the time of famine and similar other calamities special taxes were collected. Villagers repaid some traditional liabilities in the form of grains which could be measured and weighed.[162] They used to pay *Hiranya* which was synonymous[163] with gold. Artisans also had to pay something towards tax.[164] Traders had to pay "*Shulk*" for crossing the boundary which were fixed and collected by the officers posted on the border.[165] This officer had to maintain relations with businessmen, traders, artisans and corporations. Such corporations were very active in *Basarh (Vaishali), Bhita, Bulandsahar, Mandsaur,* etc.

On the basis of law books of Gupta period and land transactions of Bengal, the share of the king or state was not more than one-sixth of the crop produce during this period. Emergency taxes proposed and recommended in "*Arthashastra*" was not traceable in Gupta period. It seems Guptas' did not have a large contingent of officers, therefore, in their place stood feudal lords of donation beneficiaries, in which they were included *Brahmins, Kshatriyas,* ruling class and some other people. Among tax payers were *Vaishyas,* traders and on the bottom was exploited, suppressed working class who were mostly *Shudras.* A good part of tax was *beggar,* who was the appropriate symbols of exploited people. This was the reason for the reduction in the names of number of taxes, this was the secret. *Vakataka* inscriptions mention more taxes imposed compared to Gupta inscriptions. Revenues were mostly collected in the form of commodities.[166] Rich farmers probably paid in cash because gold coins of this period have been recovered in very large numbers and this was used in the purchase of lands. The officer collecting taxes in cash was called "*Samudayik*". An inscription obtained from Bengal belongs to early 6th century AD.[167] Alongwith *Audrangik,* this has been used, and therefore, very clearly his work would have been to collect taxes.

Main sources of land revenue were from agricultural produce only, which was sometimes called "*Bhag*". For special tax on land "*Bhag*"[168] word was first brought into used by "Kautilya".[169] At one place independently "Bali", "Kar" words are found mentioned. Under the heading "Another Country",[170] this has been used with produce,[171] *Bhag* was not to be one-sixth of produce. *Bhag* was one of the main taxes of Gupta period. In Junagarh inscription of Rudradaman, direction has been given to fill-up state treasury by *Bali Shulk* and *Bhag* and the construction of Sudarshan lake to be completed without taking any tax, *Vishti, Pranay,* has been mentioned. Along with these taxes, *Bhag* has not been described. This tax was taken only as land revenue, or this was understood to be king's share in agricultural production.

In the inscriptions of Gupta's feudal lord "*Bhag*" word has been found used coupled with *Bhog.*[172] According to archaeological and literary sources of Gupta period only a small bit of lands amongst the land donated to *Brahmins* were free from *Bhag-Bhog.*[173] '*Bhag-Bhog*' taken together as one, Fleet has used *Bhog or Ansh.*[174] In *Smritis* also '*Bhag*' or its synonym "*Ansh*" has been mentioned as land-tax.[175] According to *Shukraniti*' *Bhag* was one among the nine sources of revenues of the state. Even in Gupta period, it was taken as land-tax or received as a share of the king from produce. Thus,

Bhag-Bhog was the name of a different type of tax, easily, this can be inferred.

According to Seletor, *Bhog* has been mentioned in the Manusmiriti.[176] Commentator *Sarvagyaanarayan* has mentioned it as a daily gift of flower,-fruits, vegetables, grass, etc. Such descriptions were given by commentator keeping in mind that the dedication of '*Bhog*' to Gods' Foolish land-owners came out of their villages and stood on the way in the leadership of elderly people lifting pitchers full of water pushing each other. They come in front of the army with presents of curd, sugar, sweets and flowers and started begging for protecting their crops,' stated Banabhatta in his book 'Harsha Charit. Seletor has concluded that this *'Bhog'* was in practice during the period of Harsha.[177] He has also said it to be popular amongst *Rashtrakutas.*[178] Besides these perhaps '*Bhog*' was such a tax which was called '*gram-maryad*'[179] in Vakataka sources. In fact '*Bhog*' also was a regular tax like '*Bhag*'. In lieu of the use of royal land whatever tax was collected that was called '*Bhog*'.[180]

Besides these 'Bali' was quite important tax. According to Macdonald and Keith, this was a tax which began with the beginning of nature and was imposed on the subjects, to pay and not to pay tax did not depend on subjects. According to Arthashastra, Bali used to be the common share of the king in production.[181] According to Milindapanho, 'Bali' was a tax imposed during emergency.[182] It has been kept in the category of religious taxes. According to Maity this was imposed on *'Karu'* (Bitter) and 'Sangya' land end was a religious tax what was even imposed on even land donation during Gupta period.[183]

According to Junagarh inscription of Rudradaman also, Bali was a form of tax. Along with this there is description of revenue related other words also. In the state treasury vocabulary of Gupta period 'Bali' word has been cited for five types of taxes. In ancient Indian land-revenue system, 'Bali' word was in use for past centuries. In other literary books 'Bali' has been used as a prominent tax, but not *Bhag* in the same way.[184] Brihaspati has also described Bali in the same way. In 5th century AD in Amarkosh, it has been mentioned as a synonym of "*Shulk*" and *Kar*.[185]

Like these taxes, *Hiranya* was another form of land revenue. UN Ghoshal had said that *Hiranya* was a tax imposed on commercial crops. According to an inscription of 592 AD, sugar cane was cultivated on a particular land on which 32 silver coins were imposed as taxes. On land donated for religious purposes two and half silver coins were imposed as taxes.[186] *Hiranya* was a tax of special type which was imposed on commercial crops. According to DN Jha, there was no tax on irrigation, because the main responsibility of the state was to fulfil the need of irrigation.

In state treasury words, *Uparikar and Udrang* are important. We find its description only in Gupta period inscriptions, not in any other sources[187] of post-Maurya period. According to Fleet, *Uparikar* is made of two words *Uparikar* and *Madhyam*. This tax was taken from those farmers who had no rights whatsoever on land. In this regard, L.D. Bernet has struck down the views of Ghoshal. He says that *Uparikar* is a word resembling Tamil. In Sanskrit, Bengali languages, *Uparikar* has been interpreted as additional tax.

According to UN Ghoshal, *Udrang* was collected from permanent farmers whereas *Uparikar* was taken from temporary peasants. *Uparikar* is formed of Marathis word "*Upari*" which means such peasants, who are not related with the village, but stayed there temporarily, where they used to go from time to time to perform agricultural works. According to Altekar, *Uparikar* was a type of tax similar to *Bhog* where in tax was paid in kind.[188] But according to D.N. Jha both of these views do not look proper in the context of this period.[189] *Uparikar* was taken only from a type of settled subjects in the form of levy.[190] And he only used to distribute lands amongst subjects. *Udrang* word means water tax. But the views of Ghoshal do not look correct. Karitalai copper plate (493-494 AD) of Maharaja Jayanath mentions that *Uparikar and Udrang* cannot be any additional tax. Halikar was taken as any special type of tax for measuring the plot in some form. In course of time, tax on land was imposed on the basis of the area. Even in fertile areas too peasants were forced to plough the fields of landowners and do several other works. In the entire Gangetic area, this was known as *'Hari' and Begari.* For Hari, Halikakar[191] (ploughing fix) word was used in medieval period and for *Begari, Vishti* was used out of which *Baith-Begari* word was being used.

In the inscriptions of some feudal lords of Gupta Bhoot, pratyay has been used. Alterkar has described it as a tax on objects that will come to existence.[192] According to this, it was a tax on things to be manufactured in the state. From some inscriptions, we come to know that even artisans had to pay some taxes and from traders also,[193] on the materials of trade *chungi* (octroi) was taken which was fixed and collected by *chungi* (octroi) officers.[194] Among other taxes *Divya, Meghva, Dhanya*, etc., was also there.[195] Description of *Divya* is found in the Surat inscription of king Vyaghrasen, which means something to be given. Its description is found in Sarvaditya *Visthi's Pariharan* which means excluding all taxes on forced labour – all types of taxes were imposed. Description of Megha is found in western and central part of state treasury documents. In Madhuvan copper plate inscription of Harsha,[196] we find a *Haranya* description of Megha, which has been used as an adjective of *Bhag and Bhog.* According to this description, one thing that could be weighed or measured, revenue of the king was nominal. In the documents of this period nowhere with *Bhag, Bhogkar,* etc., Meya has been described. In most of the land grant chanters in place of *Bhog, Bhegkar "Dhanya Bhogkar'* has been used. It is clear from this that Dharsen-II- *'Swadhanya Bhog Bhag Hiranyadeva'* has been described. By this *Bhag, Bhog* and *Dhanya* can be compared. In view of Ghoshal Dhanya was definite amount of tax, where as '*Bhag*' was a definite part of produce.[197]

Sometimes, king used to take cow and bullocks for ploughing government lands. Therefore, a donation Katta-Bhatta was sometimes denied. According to Buhler, in order to get government lands permanently ploughed sometimes peasants were allowed such privileges. Bhagwan Lal Indraji has taken this to mean Katta-Bhatta. The police kept against robbers in order to feed them Katta-Bhatta was taken. This was taken to keep Government servants always pleased. People used to collect Katta-Bhatta from the land that was sold, villagers considered them as hated people. In general sense, Katta-Bhatta was an unnecessary tax. This was collected for those government officials, who did guarding jobs, collected revenues and caught thieves.

During Gupta period, taxes were collected from peasants and other citizens also. In Sivani donation inscription of Pravarsen and Khoh donation inscription of Jayanath and in Amarkosh *Shulk (chungi)* has been described.

In Pillar inscription of Bihar, an officer named *Shaulkik* (cone who collected *shulka)* has been discussed and in an essay of Dharmaditya and Vyaparkaranya (Controller of trade) has been discussed.[198] This was to be paid on *Ghat (Ghatta Dideya)* and on the city gate. Narad has provided detailed laws regarding *Shulk.*[199] He has kept *Brahmins* free from taxes even if they be engaged in trading.[200] Just in the same way, he gives opinion on suddenly found wealth in land that *varnas* should hand it over to the king but a *Brahmin* could retain such wealth.[201] In inscriptions, after the land has been donated if any wealth, mine and salt, is found there in that land that will belong to the king but at times king used to forgo his rights on these. Descriptions *klipt and upaklipt* are found in four *Vakataka* donation letters. Ghoshal and Ram Shastri accept them as a definite tax and DC Sarkar calls it sales tax. Maity did not take it as tax rather he takes it as a related defining word with 'Bhogawadhi'. One source of the income of the state was fines collected from the thieves, right to collect that was given to the receivers of land donation at times by the king.[202] According to Fa-hien during Gupta period, though the amount of crimes was less yet at times offenders had to be rewarded with financial punishments. This also was a source of income of the king but its amount was very less.

In inscriptions of Pallavas, there is mention of land donation was given from eighteen *'Parihaths'*.[203] But it was not counted.[204] The descriptions of land donation arrangements have been clearer in this period than before. There are two inscriptions related to modern Indore out of which is one of Maharaja Swamidas (396-387 AD) and another Maharaj Bhurpada[205] (426-427AD). There is description of land donated to Brahmins, because here land-owners receiving land in donation have been shown. In the rural economic system, there was provision of implementing several taxes related to land revenue which were borne by the inhabitants of the village.

During Gupta period like earlier days 1/6th part of the produce was given to the king, and it has been called *'Shadbhagin'*.[206] According to Kalidas, king was entitled to one-sixth part of the land produce. Kalidas has also written that hermits also were to pay one-sixth part of their repentance to the king.[207] And one-sixth part of the rice accumulated by them on the bank of river side by them was to be handed over to the royal officers of the state.

Fa-Hien has also given information about some new taxes. Kamandak had also framed some new laws which reduced the burden of taxes on common masses. Fa-Hien has written that sometimes when someone was unable to pay some new taxes, he had to leave the town and take shelter along the border of the state. But no clear description is available for this. Though indirect incidents, it was assumed that in the situation of non-payment of taxes by the peasants they had to live their village and had to take shelter in the donated villages.[208] The king used to warn such receivers of donations not to allow any such person to enter their village, who has not paid taxes in the past in the state treasury and whose land has been taken back on this count. By the descriptions of Fa-Hien, it is known that only those who were doing agricultural work paid a certain part of their produce to the kind.[209] Besides land taxes, those who produced sugar and indigo state tax was imposed on them *Smritis* of earlier times also said that in exchange of taxes king was entitled to get one-day '*Begar*'.

Other sources of revenue were land-gems, buried secret wealth, mines, salt, etc. Some lands were under the direct ownership of the king properly gained by the sale proceeds of that were a source of income. At times someone found out some property buried under the soil. But of them excluding the case of *Brahmin,* rest of it belonged to the king if they were found by people of other *varnas* by the time of his death, and who had no heir-apparent that used to pass on to king.[210] Feudal lords and king below presented gifts to the king which increased the income of the king.[211] Samudra Gupta after winning the kingdom of south and when he set them free they gave presents to Samudra Gupta in return.[212] Just like this, king of Sinhala Island for constructing vihar in Bodh Gaya had given presents to the rulers of Pataliputra.[213]

In Gupta period, there were certain laws for the payment of taxes. According to Narada, in order to pay sale tax and Octroi, business men had to go to the post and pay the taxes. Those who violated this law and showed wrong datas about sale, did not reveal correct account of sale, he had to pay eight times towards penalty. From a coin of Vaishali Ranabhandegaradhikaran has come to be known. It is clear from this source that army revenue department and general department were separate.

There was very well-organised plan for spending the income received from taxes. According to Kalidas, Gupta rulers collected taxes only in the interest and for the benefit of their subjects.[214] After looking into the income only a plan was prepared for expenditure.[215] According to Fa-Hien, the employees of Gupta period were on pay. Therefore, an important item of the expenditure of the state used to be paid. On the basis of inscriptions, it is known that Gupta rulers did general welfare works i.e., digging canal, constructing schools, etc. *Brahmins* got *Agrahar* donations from this in the interest of the state. For emergency situations, king used to save some property out of this and kept it. It has been called "Vyaya-Pratyaya'.[216] Economic condition of the general masses was not very good because many new taxes were laden on them. Several economic units are seen which was the logical culmination of decentralised tax system. In all the donations of Gupta period various forms of revenues have been discussed, but '*Udrang'* and *uparikar* of Gupta period were not beyond confusion.

Holistically, it can be said that feudal system expanded on a large scale during Gupta period. In feudal society, there was dominance of Brahmins and higher castes. From feudal society, it is known that in the list of privileges, *Brahmin-*

Kshatriya classes held the highest position and the king was in reality their protector only. Among *Vaishya* castes wealthiers and traders combined together with high castes and used to exploit working class. Other *Vaishyas and Shudra* community were completely oppressed and suppressed. This social structure continued to remain in India.

References

1. Aitarey Bhrahman : VIII 21; Satpath Brahman; VIII.7.1.15; VIII.1.18:1.73.4; Chhandogya Upanishad IV.2.4-5; Cambridge history of India, Vol. I, Ed. Rapson, page 1.1.118.
2. Abastamb Dharmsutra II.10.26 (i); Gautam Dharmasutra V.19; XIX.16: Vasisth Dharmasutra XXVIII-16, XXIX, 19.
3. Manu Smriti IV.230.
4. Mahabharata III.199.127ff; Mahabharata Shantiparva 12.31; 35.19.
5. Apastanb Dharmasutra II.10.26;1;Vishnusmriti III.81.
6. Arthasastra II.12; XUUU.5.
7. Arthasastra II.2.
8. Epigraphia Indica, VII.57ff; VIII,78 ff and 86; Select Inscription, Vol I, Ed DC Sarkar. Calcutta 160f; 165ff: LL, 1099, 1131, 1135, Indian antiquity, 1883 Vol VII, page 24 ff.
9. Epigraphia Indica, VI 84ff; Select inscription, 453, LL no 1205.
10. Epigraphia Indica, 1, page 55 ff, 9 ff; 479, II, 485 fl VI, 88; Select Inscriptions, page 188, LII, LL No 1112.
11. Epigraphia Inidica, VI, 31 ff; LL No 1328.
12. Select Inscriptions, page 188, LII, LL No 1112.
13. Epigraphia Indica, VIII, 78 ff, Select inscriptions, 162f, LL No 1131.

14. S Chattopadhyaya, The Shakas in India, page 40.
15. Epigraphia Indica, XX page 16, 19ff; XXI.62: Select inscriptions page 219-20, II, 4.5, page 227, 1.1, page 229, UU 3-4, page 230, 1.6.
16. Suttanipat, 5.1, 978; Jatak, III. 428 ff; Jatak, III 104, 229; Jatak IV.473, 98 ff; Jatak, Nos 542, 546, Vimanvatthu, 332, 337.
17. Arthasastra II, I; III.10.
18. Epigraphia Indica, VI.84.
19. Suttanipat, V.1.978. No 442.
20. Epigraphia Indica, VIII 71, VIII, 73 ff; select inscription, 191 ff, 193 ff.
21. Epigraphia, VII, 61ff; select inscriptions, 133f, LL No. 1100.
22. Epigraphia Indica, VIII, VIII, 60ff; VIII, 67; Select inscriptions, 196ff; 200ff.
23. Epigraphia Indica, VIII, 78ff; VII, 57ff; LL No 1131, LL No 1099.
24. Jatak, 1.85.
25. Epigraphia Indica, VIII, 65.
26. Mahavastu, 111; 114ff; cf Milindpanho, 279; Thergatha 957.
27. Jatak, 192f; Anguttar Nikay; V page 1.
28. Dhampada Kavya; III.246..
29. Mahavastu, I.295.
30. Mahavastu, I.300:293.
31. Same.
32. Arthashastra II.I.
33. Same, II. XI.
34. Mahavastu, II. 123.
35. Manusmriti VII. 119.
36. Mahabharat, XIII. 87, 6-8.

37. Jatak, I, 364ff, 441, III, 104; IV. 413; VI 261, 363.
38. Arthasastra II.1.
39. Same, II: 1.
40. Ramayan II. 31.22.
41. Jatak, II.237, 403; IV.342ff; IV.80.
42. Arthasastra II.35.
43. Epigraphia Indica, VIII, 78f, 86; VII, 58.
44. LL No 1195; (Luders List of Brahmi Inscriptions, Journal of the Royal Asiatic Society of Great Britain and Ireland, 1905, page 304.
45. Epigraphia Indica, VIII, 143ff; Select Inscription, 443ff, LL No 1327.
46. Arthasastra, II 20.
47. Jatak, I.138, Jatak, No 541 (Nimi Jatak).
48. Ghoshal, Agrarian System in Ancient India, Page 27f.
49. Jatak, 1.420.
50. Same, VI.344.
51. Manusmriti, II. 245-6.
52. Epigraphia Indica, VIII, 92; LL No 1142.
53. Epigraphia Indica, viii, 78-9; select inscriptions, 162, 1.4.
54. Jatak, 1.92ff.
55. Rani (Allahabad) Pillar inscriptions, DC Sarkar.
56. Epigraphia Indica, VIII, 143ff; select inscriptions, 443ff.
57. Mahavastu, 1.295,300; Secred Boooks of the East XI, page 59; Jatak, V.44.
58. Naradsmriti, 1.26.
59. Select Inscriptions, page 194, II.3-4.
60. Luders List, No 1196.
61. Journal of the Royal Asiatic Society of Great Briatain And Ireland, 1905, page 305.

62. Arthasastra III, 16, Manusmriti; VIII.199, Yagyavalkya Smriti; II.160.
63. Manusmriti, VIII.165.
64. Epigraphia Indica, 1.page 5ff, 479; II 485; VI.88.
65. Vishnusmriti III.82.
66. Epigraphia Indica, VIII, 72.
67. Same VI, 88.
68. Same VI. 315ff.
69. Same VIII, 72f; 65ff.
70. Same VI, 315ff
71. Same, VIII, 72f; VII, 65ff.
72. Same I, page 5ff, 9ff, 479; II, 483f; VI, 88f.
73. Same VII, 61 Kerla, Babddha Gaha Lakh.
74. Jatak, IV 247.
75. Same, No 446.
76. Luders list, Ed.1099, 1131, 1135, Jatak, vi. 261, 363.
77. Epigraphic Indica VII, 65; VIII.72.
78. Indian Antiquity, 1910, page 200-201, Dharmadityas second letter.
79. Epigraphia Indica 1910, page 193-216.
80. Indian antiquary 1910, page 192-216.
81. Indian History quarterly, IV, page 53-55.
82. Fleet, page 254, Epigraphia Indica, XXV, page 50.
83. Same, page 47.
84. Same, page 52.
85. Journal of the Asiatic Society of Bengal, XX, page 53.
86. Hastina Khoh plate, Fleet, page 93, 106, Sankshobh's Khoh plate, Fleet page 112. Jayanath's Khoh plate, Fleet, page 125; Jayanath's Karitalai plate, Fleet page-117.

87. Chandragupta's Sanchi Inscription, Fleet, page-29.
88. Dharmdditya's plate 2. Inidan antiquity, 1910 page 29.
89. Journal of the Asiatic Society of Bewngol, XX, page 53; Epigraphic Indica, XI, page 39.
90. Fleet, page 164, 121, 125, 129, 135.
91. Damodarpur plate, 1; Indian antiquity, 1910, page 193.
92. Fleet, page 164, 171, 191, 231 and 243.
93. Hastin's Khok plate, Fleet 93 and 100; Samudra Gupta's Gaya plate, page 254; Samudra Gupta's Nalanda plate, Epigraphia Indica Vol 25, page 50; Jayanath's Karitalai plat Fleet, page 117.
94. Fleet, page 235.
95. Same, page 243.
96. Sarvanath's Khoh plate- Fleet page 129, 125; Sankshobh's khoh plate –fleet, page 112.
97. Fleet, page 29.
98. Same, page 241-242.
99. Same, page 132.
100. Naradasmriti, IV.6 and Brihaspatismriti XIV.3.
101. Brihaspatismriti, XIV.5.
102. Same, XIV.6.
103. Naradasmriti IV, 9-11 and Brihaspatismriti, XIV 15-17.
104. Brihaspati smriti, XIV. 17.
105. Naradsmriti, IV.12.
106. Ramsharan Sharma, Prarambhik Bharat Ka Arthik Aur Samajik Itihas, Hindi Madhyam Karyanway Nideshalaya, Dwitiya Sansakaran, 1993, page.
107. Select inscriptions bearing on Indian History and Civilisation page 445-46, Moolpath, page 26-29.

108. Raghuvansh, XVII. 66.
109. II, III Select inscription, page 442, Moot path, page 29.
110. Journal of Bihar Research Society, XXXIX, page 32.
111. The Nandanpur Copper plate inscriptions of Gupta Era, page 169.
112. Select inscriptions I, page 422, Moolpath, page 40-43.
113. Epigraphia Indica, XV, 5-11.
114. KJVirji, Ancient History of Saurastra, pages 47, 267.
115. Naradasmriti, XIII. 38.
116. Brihaspatismriti; XXVI, 10, 28, 43, 53, 64.
117. Corpus Inscriptionum Indicarum, IV Introduction, CIXXI.
118. Legge, A Record of Bauddhistic Kingdom, page 43.
119. Corus inscription, XXVI,10, 28, 53, 64.
120. Legge, a record of bhuddhistic kingdom , page 42, 43.
121. Same, II, 158.
122. Yyagyavalkya smriti,II. 157.
123. Same, II.158.
124. Brihaspatismrti,II. 157.
125. Yagyavalkya smriti, II.157, Brihastismriti, XIX.19.53-55.
126. Rigard X.173.6.
127. Aitreya Brahman: VIII,29; Satpath Brahman: XI.2.6.14.
128. Same II,29.
129. Atharvaveda,II.29.
130. Ram sharan Sharma,prachin bharat me rajanitik vihar Avam.
131. Katyayanasmriti Sansthayen, page 115, shloka 16.
132. Naradasmriti, 18.46.
133. Kamandak nitisar, 6.46.
134. Same, 5.85.

135. Raghuvansh, 1.18.
136. Shi Ram Goyal, Gupta samragya ka itihas page 401.
137. C.1., 3.
138. hasti ka jhajhawan danapatra same page 107.
139. Dikshitar, Hindu administrative system, page104.
140. praja Nameva Bhootyaratha satabhyo balim grathita, Raguvanshi, 1.18.
141. Ram sharam sharman, above refered page 370.
142. Sarkar, Same page 272.
143. Same page 213.
144. J.A.S.B., 1911.
145. S.K. Maity, above referred, page 87.
146. Manusmrite 7.138.
147. C.I.I, page 2, page 238.
148. A.S. Altekar Rastrakutas and their time, page 229, Hindu revenue system, page 227.
149. Manusmriti, 8.4.
150. Leggo, page 42.3.
151. Radhakrishra Chaudhary above referred page,212.
152. S.K. Maity above referred, page 401.
153. Same.
154. Shri Ram Goyal, above referred, page 77.
155. Manusmriti, 7.130-32.
159. Raghuvansh, 1.45, 5.41.
160. Shri Ram Goyal above referred page 402.
161. Fleet, Gupta inscriptions, no. 23, 26, 28.
162. Ka. E.E. 3.60 line 12.
163. A.E,13 E line 3.
164. Same.
165. Same ed 12, pine 29.

166. Ram Sharm Sharma above referred, page 310.
167. S.E.3, ed line 4.
168. D.N Jha revenue system in post Maurya and Gupta times, page 42.
169. A.S, 2.6.
170. Same, 2.15.
171. Some hindu physical terms discussed, page 203.
172. K.E.E.3, page 132.
173. C.E, 326, 1.27 1.11.
174. Same, page 259, P.T.
175. Gautam smriti, 10. 24-27, Manu smriti 8.130.
176. Manu smriti 8.5.
177. Harsh charit, page III.
178. E.A.II, page III.
179. K.E.E. 3.
180. Parmeshwarilal Gupta, above referred, page 402.
181. U.N. Ghosal above referred, page ?
182. Milind panho, page 146.
183. S.K. Maity above referred, page 61.
184. Brihaspati smriti, 2.20.
185. Amarkosh 2.8.2.8.
186. E.I. 15.140-30.
187. C.E.
188. Altekar, above referred, page, 216.
189. D.N. Jha above referred, page 54.
190. C.E. 2.3, No. 26, 11.8-10.9.
191. U.N. Ghoshal above referred page 210.
192. S.K. Maity, above referred page 62.
193. Same.
194. Rajitarangini, page 291-292.
195. The Sohewal copper plates of the year, 191,1.10.

196. U.N Ghosal, above referred page 213.
197. S.K. Maity above referred, page 63.
198. Y.B singh Halikakar; Crystalisation of the practice into a tax Indian history congress, 1982 Krukshetra.
199. Vakatak Gupta age, page 291.
200. A.E. 28 Ed-8, page 2.
201. Same Ed 12, page 29.
202. E.I., 11, No. 21.
203. Madhuban Inscription, 7.22.1.17.
204. U.N Ghosal, above referred, page 219.
205. Sri Ram Goyal above referred page 219.
206. Narada smriti 8.12-19.
207. Same 18.38.
208. Same 7.6-7.
209. Shri Ram Goyal, above referred page 403.
210. D.N. Jha above referred page 38.
211. Select inscription page 439-40.
212. I.I 15.16.
213. Vishnu smriti 9.22.
214. Raguvansha, 2.26.
215. The Spuryas Gaya plate of Smudra Gupta page 257.
216. Travels of Fa-Hien, page 42-43.

3

Peasant Society

Peasants are important elements of social structure. By telling peasant society, such a society is expressed immediately which is combining itself with village or rural life and joins agriculture as occupation. Historians have been lacking in viewing peasant independently from rural community. Nature of ancient literary sources also being nobility-oriented hindrances have been coming in the way of study of peasant. In Brahmanic books of ancient times have attempted to observe rural life and city life separately. As for example, these *Brahmin* books of three types can be *Dharmashastra*, *Arthasastra* and *Kamsutra*. In first type of books i.e., in *Dharmshastra* and *Smriti* literature, rural life has been depicted and to this extent it has been told about rural life that in rural life only one can live a pure, clean, honest and peaceful life and in that way obey religious[1] duties. Elsewhere *Arthashastra* written by Kautilya and *Kamasutra* written by Vatsyayan are initial books supporting different type of ideology. From *Arthasastra*, we get to know only about city because of its city-centric thought (ideology) and about rural structure.

Vatsyayan go one step further ahead in very clear words to say that to live and to live worth living town alone is the appropriate place.[2] From the works of Kalidas and Bhas also we come to know of the same ideology. Reflections of time and space can be seen on those treatises.[3]

Thus, traditional Sanskrit literature is necessary to understand initial stages of society – so far as *Dharmashastras* are concerned, despite village supportive ideology, it has neither tried to understand contemporary rural peasant organisation nor attempted to carve out its image completely. From this point of view in shape, it is as much nobility-oriented and away from peasant society, as other important writings like *Arthasastra or Kamsutra*. According to Raffel Samuels, Social history in its true senses gains its live-energy from contradictory characters.

It takes pride in combining real-life, more than compared to any ideology, combining with common masses more than combining with nobility, linking with daily incidents rather than some hairs raising incidents. In ancient India, rural society was not only divided into social classes rather it was defined even on the basis of geography. On this basis of an individual it was divided into dynasty, *gotra, caste* and *varna*. These only divided in these situations like house, village, city, town, subject and country.

In order to do agricultural works the role of labourer was very important. The labourers have to do all kinds of job for good good crops production. According to Rigveda, Aswin was the first man who performed labourious ploughing job for agriculture.[4] Prithuvainya has been described as the first agricultural-scientist in Atharveda.[5] Therefore, these categories (1) Keenas and Krishiwal (man ploughing field) (2) Gopa and Gopal (cattle tender), (3) Avipal and Ajapal (goat rearer), (4) Pushup (Shepherd), (5) Dhanyakrit worker for cleaning paddy),

(6) Upalprashani (worker cleaning husk from the grain, and (7) Bap (worker sowing seeds) etc find their mention in Vedas as agricultural labourers.

Aryans were also peasant. Therefore, people in Vedic age had interest in agriculture. At one place, gamblers have been well-advised to do agricultural works and shun gambling. Though, this be can definitely gain wife, property and cattle.[6] This saying explains the social criticism of these days and denounces tendencies like gambling. Gradually, big land owners came up who started keeping many peasants for their agricultural works. Along with this, the number of such persons also grew who had no lands at all and who survived on the labour, they did on the fields of other. Hence, it is natural that in order to meet their both ends, they squarely depended on labour. Such slave women have been described in the Atharvaveda, who cleaned paddy in Okhali (mortar)[7] with the help of Musal (pestle), who survived squarely on their labour.

Such agriculture related works for obtaining grains on any workers were kept. Cattle tenders of Vedic age used to take away cattle for tending them in the morning and in the evening.[8] They returned them safe. A main quality of the cattle tender was to always keep an eye on the cattle and bring them back providing protection to them to the residence. God Pushan was the protectors of cattle, who protected the cattle.[9] In later literatures like Dharmsatras which came up in later period, it has been mentioned that if there was any damage to any cattle of the grazing ground tender was to be punished.[10] If any tender returned the cattle without any prior intimation to the owner, then it was punishable.[11] Law had provided that if any cattle was stolen or damaged due to carelessness of the tender, he had to compensate it to the master on account of his carelessness.[12]

In Buddhist literature, there are several such descriptions which give information related with master and servants. In those days, rich *Brahmins* also used to be farmers, they possessed hundreds of ploughs and bullocks for ploughing fields. Such *Brahmins* besides themselves employed several men for labour.[13] To the contrary, there were so may *Brahmins* who due to poverty, were living the life of peasants and ploughed their lands with only one bullock.[14] In the society of those days, the number of labourers and servants were very large. Officers of the state of land were generally *Kshatriyas or Brahmins,* who employed servants to complete agricultural works. Workers received their wages from them on rosters in the form of either cash or grain in any form[15] which they spent on themselves and their family for their very sustenance. According to Kautilya, wage was paid to the workers in the form of grain. In case the wage was not decided, they were given one-tenth of the total produce.[16] But looking at the amount of labour done by the workers, their wage was very less.[17] It is known from the Jatakas that wage paid workers after doing work during the day-time returned to their houses by the evening.[18] It was considered to work from morning to evening almost as their religion.[19] Along with them even women workers remained busy with their works in the field.[20] According to the literature of those days that nearly four types of servants kept on serving; (a) daily wage earning labourers, (2) workers kept for travelling related works on contract, (3) daily workers on contract basis, and (4) workers kept by the master to work inside the house as well as outside the house for different works.

Panini has discussed a number of agricultural operations in ploughing, sowing, harvesting, and thrashing.[21] These were almost entirely completed with the help of peasants. Patanjali, further says that one who purchased labour (owner) was called "Artha".[22] One who bought for certain amount individual labour for certain period was known by the 'awakreta'. For the period of one year, two years or for a period even more than that one paid one hundred, five hundred or one thousand *karshapan* and kept a labourer as servant for work.[23] Names of these categories of workers were decided on the period they were kept. Servants getting five, six or seven or ten *karshapans* were called in the same order Panchaka, Saptaka, Dashaka or were known by the name Panchaka Masik, Saptaka Masik or Dasheka Masik.[24] A teacher who was appointed to teach for an hour or two was known as a monthly teacher, and any worker who worked daily for some hours, he was called monthly worker.[25]

There were some such workers also in the society, who got full wages but did not indulge in work whole-heartedly. Such workers on the arrival of their masters looked at neck and foreheads and then started working, otherwise they did not work, and they were called "*Lalatik Shramik*". To the contrary, there were also such workers who worked very slowly, they were known as "*sheetak*". Such workers who worked intelligently and fastly were know as "*ushnak*".[26]

For the protection of works not only the people but even the king used to remain very conscious. At one place in Mahabarata, Narada asked Yudhisthir "in your state do you pay attention towards workers. The enrichment of the state depends on the co-operation of the workers only".[27] A description almost similar to this is found in Ramayana too, when Rama asks Bharat "Are the people depending on agriculture and animal husbandry in your state enjoying their life? Are you able to fulfil their needs and make efforts to do away with their difficulties?" The main duty (work) of the king is to protect his subjects without any discrimination.[28] It seems that in initial stages of Gupta period, the condition of the workers was not stable. Due to this in Ramayana in one context the Ram said that it was a matter of deep sorrow that workers in the state are neither paid their wages nor food in time which makes their condition painful and this is the cause of their deplorable condition.[29] At times, we get even evidences which make it clear that the conditions of the workers were quite high in the society and they were respected at par with parents and *Brahmins.*[30]

People engaged in agriculture and animal husbandry were considered well-contented and happy in the field of farming activities and in order to satisfy their needs, they worked continuously in the field for crops production which is utmost importance for the peasants and landless labourers for their susrvival. Narad has written that in the absence of land-owner, other people could cultivate his land. During this period, if the land-owner returned he could plough the cost of ploughing etc., and could get back his land. But if the land-owner is not resourceful enough to pay these amount backs in seven yearly instalments from crop produce from the land and on eight years the land was handed over to the land-owner.[31] According to Yagyavalkya, one-tenth of the crop produced was paid to the workers who worked on it.[32] But in the early medieval period the condition of the workers improved Devannabhatta in his book Smritichandrika has made it clear that one-tenth of the produced on which the crop has been produced with too much of labour. According to him workers should get food and clothes also from the owner of the land, if food and clothes could not be provided workers should be given one- third of the crop produce.[33] This statement indicates that the high-level of the workers usually it was observed that ill paid workers behave in a bitter way worth their masters. Workers were given fifteen days paid holidays yearly. Besides this they were given holidays on illness and they also received *Niwritti kosh* (retirement benefits), if a worker remained sick for very long period, he was given wage for over three months. While commenting on Manusmriti, Medhatithi says that in every month, one drona weight of grain and a piece of cloth in every six months should be given towards wage to every common worker and on the basis it he should be paid in every month.[34]

Ancient Hindu Dharmshastra writer's opinion related to workers reflects their social situation. Some writers have expressed their opinion on human basis and banned exploitation of the workers of land-owners or landlords. But in practical life, workers had to face many restrictions and angers. Most of the time, they were compelled to lead a life of responsibilities.

Citing Katyayana Chandeshwar says that unclean jobs should not get to be done by the workers. Regarding this, he has submitted a long list which includes clear roads, doors of the houses getting collected and left over of meals getting them and thrown even.[35]

Foundation stone of the society was *varna* system while caste system was prevalent. Efforts were made to restrain various castes within the ambit of their duties. King was supposed to be the protector of society, he directed caste organisation. It was his duty to stop illegal mixing of hybridisation. In a Gupta inscription provincial ruler Abhaydata was described as protector of caste and his son was described as one who stopped the mixing of caste.

Vanished Vedic traditions again had come to life and importance of *Varnashram dharma* had started growing up. In social organisation, four *varnas in Brahmans, kshatriya, Vaishyas and Shudra* and four *Ashramas brahacharya, grihastha, vanaprastha and sanyas* once again had re-established, their importance. All classes were carefully doing their duties. People belonging to various *varnas* were respected on the basis of adherence and obedience to their duties. People belonging to *Brahin varna* reading and teaching and doing sacrifice or performing sacrifices for others, *Kshatriyas* in *kshatra* religion and protecting subjects, *Vaishyas* in agriculture and commerce and trading and *Shurdras* were engaged in the service of the society respectively. *Brahmins* compared to other *varnas* were seen with more respect and regard because they mostly lead intellectual and spiritual life. In order to attain *siddhi* and *moksha* (salvation) they did thinking and deeper thinking. Some involved themselves in very difficult penances. They were expert in Vedic knowledge, *mantras, sutras,* commentaries, descriptions and delivering speeches on religious matters for which they were given lands and villages in donation. Like *Brahmins, Kshatriyas* also completed their duties with full commitment qualification and devotion and care they paid particular attention in nursing the subjects and protecting them. *Vaishyas* practiced trade, commerce agriculture and animal husbandry and helped enrich the country, *Shudras* also according to their strength served the society they also did other professions as well.

During Gupta period change of *Varna* and profession was possible. People belonging to *Brahimn* and artisan also worked as soldiers and *Kshatriyas* earned prestige by doing trading works. Then *Shudras* were not only confined to serving rather they worked as traders and farmers. It indicates that the occupations in different stratas of the society were not strictly determined by the castes. In this age, the condition of *Shudras* was better. Some *Shudras* were soldiers and some were even military officers. Therefore, due to applicable provision and liberty to choose professions in order to living, there was enough central unity and dynamism in the society.

The unity of society was a combined family *Smriti* books of this age and have lauded the tradition of combined family. In the inscriptions of Gupta period, there is mention of the tradition on combined family. Head of the family used to be father, elder; he carried out social and religious works of the family and also did contribution in the interest of the family.

On the other hand, astrologer Varahmihir of last quarter of the 5th century AD to first half of the 6th century in the future forecasts made about the decline of town of Gupta period could be imagined in his book,[36] Brishatsamhita Varahmihir has discussed about the low prices of grains.[37] In the future forecasts of Varahmihir lack of rains, disease, fire, famine have been described.[38] Editor and translator of Brihatsamhita M.R. Bhatta describes fall of prices of food grains as cause disaster for peasants.[39] It has been told that peasant will have to suffer from troubles, thus forecast of food crops and rise of the country has been described in the same year.[40]

In chapter, Sasyajatakam, Varahmihir generally describes good crops and along with that also describes their destruction or their infection by harmful insects.[41] S.K. Maity has studied thoroughly the adverse affects of good and bad combination of stars and planets in this book of astrology. He has traced out so many contexts of poverty commercial losses, family destructions etc. During Gupta period, the economic conditions of many people seem to be very pathetic.[42]

Thus, society of peasants was governed by the social organisation of that time. In the early centuries of the period under study, due to a number of taxes were imposed being pathetic their social condition would be, but their condition was much better in comparison with later centuries. But from 4th to 6th and 7th century, the speciality was the expansion or rural feudal economic organisation and the development of feudal society and culture, which formed due to the gradual growth in the force of basic caste structure of Indian society. Caste was used by feudal rulers in their interest in such a way that the shape of Indian society kept on becoming more and more complex. *Brahmin, Kshatriyas* or ruler and *Purohits* joined together and broke the Indian society into castes and sub-castes and shattered it. Its negative impact affected all the aspects of life. With this inheritance *Bharatvarsh* could never be galvanised into shape of one united nation and in the cycle of history often fell victim to the aggressive powers. In the words of Baba Sahib Ambedkar, untouchability and caste system is the root cause of all these deformities which is destroying social justice. By the study of this, we come to know about the process of making of this type of social structure, and we can also get help in understanding its form.

References

1. Baudhayan Dharmasutra 11.3.6.33-34, Manusmriti, 4.213.
2. Kamsutra, 1.4.2.
3. Racfel Samuels, What is social history today, March 1985, page 34.
4. Rigveda, 8.22.6.
5. Atharvaveda, 8.10.24.
6. Rigverda, 10.34.13.
7. Atharvaveda, 12.3.13.
8. Rigveda, 10.19.5.6.
9. Same, 10.17.3.
10. Gautam Dharmasutra, 12.19.20.
11. A.Dh.Su.22.28.23.
12. Same, 28.6.
13. Suttanipat 14, 1.17 Jatak, 11.181.
14. Burligame Buddhist legends, 29.2,343.
15. Jatak, 2.3.129;326,4.50,320,5.212 etc.
16. Arthasastra 3.13.
17. Jatak, 1.475;2.325.

18. Same 3.448,446.
19. Same, 4.14,277.
20. Same, 1.11, 475, 3.446.
21. Panini, 5.2.112; 6.2187; 5.4.12.
22. Mahabhashya, 3.1.103.
23. Same, 1.4.44.,
24. Same 5.4.116.
25. Same,5.4.116.
26. Same 4.4 66;5.2.72.
27. Mahabarata, 2.100.47.48.
28. Ramayana, 2.100.47.48.
29. Same, 2.100.33.
30. Same, 2.110.13.
31. Narada smriti, 11.20-22.
32. Yogya, 2.194.
33. Smriti chandrika, 2.20
34. Medhatithi, Manu, 7.126.
35. Vivadartnakar page 40.
36. Varahminhirs page A.M. Shastri, India as seen in Brihatsamjila of Varahmihir, page 16.
37. S.K.Maity, above referred, page 195.
38. Brihatsamhita.
39. Brihatsmhita, part 1, page 35.
40. Ibid., IV, 9.
41. Ibid., XI, 1.
42. S.K. Maity, p. 190.

4

Peasant Culture

By just telling peasant culture, we get an expression of such a culture which is connected with village. Peasants are important element of social structure. Historians have been lacking in trend to see peasant separately from, village community. The nature of ancient literary sources being noble there is hindrance in studies related to peasants. In traditional *Brahmin* books, attempts have been made to see villages and towns separately. For example, the first three categories of *Brahmin* books, *Dharmasatra, Arthasaastra and Kamsutra* can be seen. First category of books *Dharma sutra* and *Smriti* literature while pleading for rural life go to the extent of saying that only in rural atmosphere a man while living pure, clean, honest, and peaceful life can comply with his religion.[1] On the other hand, *Arthasastra* written by Kautilya and *Kamsutra* written by Vatsyayana are books supporting another type of ideology? From *Arthasastra,* we get to know only about town-centric things about rural organisations. We know nothing Vatsyayana goes one step further still and say in clear words that in order to lead a worth living, town is the only appropriate place.[2] Similar opinions have been expressed from the works of Kalidas and *Bhasa*.

Thus, in order to know the ancient stage of peasant society, the study of ancient India and ancient Sanskrit literature is necessary; whereas the case of *Dharmasastras* are concerned, though it is supportive of villages, it has neither attempted to understand rural peasant organisation nor has made efforts to carve out a clear picture of the same. From this point of view, these too are in shape similarly noble and separate from peasant community as much is important books of the other ideology in *Arthasastra* and *Kamasutra* are concerned. Though in these two sources, village and towns have been described as two different forms of culture, whereas rural culture was a culture directed by miracle of religion therein the culture of towns had negligible religious impact. General speciality of rural culture was religion. This entirely depended on religion, where as town culture in the views of traditionalists was non-religious because town folks did not have any regards for *Brahmanical* values.[3] To enrage the traditionalists, it was enough therefore a sense of hatred developed in them towards the society of towns. On the other hand, it was impossible for the rural peasants living in villages to challenge religion and *Brahmanical* values.

Therefore, in order to study peasant culture in ancient India, it is very much important to understand religion, because it is religion and religious values which are used to exploit the peasants and landless labourers to the maximum possible extent.

During this period, religion was inseparably linked to peasant culture. From ancient times itself, agricultural work was related to God and thus was made pious work from ancient times only Rudra has been described as the god of forest, farm and land in ancient religious literature and it has been told that he lives inside the earth.[4] Besides this "*Langul*" *and* "*Linga*" have been used for plough and panis respectively which convey the same meaning. Since *Linga* was linked with *Shaivism,* therefore, it was supposed that Shiva was the god connected to the growth of plants.[5] According to Megasthanese,[6] in ancient times Indians were vagabonds. They did not do farming till Dionysus came and taught them ploughing and sowing, it was Greek God only who taught them yoking bull in ploughs. In ancient tales of Greece Krishi[7] (agriculture) has been combined with agricultural ritual of Dionysius who can be compared with rural Shiva as holding plough in hand Shankarshan or Baldev which has been described in the epic book,[8] when Shankarshan was combined with another gods of production i.e., Vasudev or Vishnu thereafter in various parts of the country peasants started worshipping Vishnu and Shiva. From *Arthashastra,* we come to know that before sowing a handful of grain with a piece of gold, it was washed in water and sown first of all chanting. I salute Prajapati Kashyap.[9] Let agriculture develop and goddesses live in seed and property. It is worth mentioning here that later on Kashyap was linked with Vishnu who is worshipped as the highest god and controller of the universe. This also indicates that later on Ram, who was identified with Vishnu and his wife Sita on whom fertility of soil was assumed to depend. In the same way, the left side of the statue of *Ardhanareeshwara* obtained from Mathura was identified as wife of lord Shiva by their worshippers.[10]

Strabo[11] says that Indians worshipped Jew Ombrosias (like rain). This Greek god can be identified with the god of clouds Indra described in Indian books. Peasants also worshiped bulls and other animals useful in agriculture. For increase in crop production sacrifices were performed. Classical writers[12] have mentioned that in the beginning of the every year the king convened a meeting of the religious philosophers to increase wealth in the form of grain and cattle from Buddhist literature also it is known that peasants used to contact learned Brahmins in order to know how to use new agricultural implements.[13] For ploughing fields and sowing, an auspicious[14] date and time was selected by astrologers in one Jataks,[15] a Brahmin says today is my ploughing festival. So, we consider earth or soil, cattle, and other related tools for cultivation were objects of religious or semi-religious importance. During this period, peasant culture were inseparably linked with religion and religious *karma* and (rituals). Truth is that even today Indian peasants are linked with religion and religious-type of activities in the same way. But this religious nature of the peasants in those days became the basis of their exploitation. Inseparable parts of peasant culture were, in those days, their food and drinking habits, their clothes and dressing instruments used by them for entertainment etc.

Through various literary sources, the description of food items that we produce are barley, (yava)[16] rice (shali)[17], kalma[18] varieties' of paddy and Til[19], molasses[20], gandika[21] varieties of sugar,[22] and their sweets, sweets milk,[23] and butter, ghee,[24] curd,[25] kheer,[26] honey,[27] money, various types of meat,[28] fish,[29] chilly,[30] cardamom,[31] long[32] clove, various types of spices, salt[33] and sweet[34] mango like innumerable fruits.

During these days barley, wheat and rice were the main food crops of rural people. Sugarcane and ghee were prepared from sugarcane and milk and many types of *modaks* were made by sugar. In dramas written by Kalidas, the diet in which interest is shown by Vidushakas shows the kinds of food in which common masses were interested. At a time, Vidushakas says that his stomach is burning like the pan of a sweet-maker on fire.[35] It can be said on the basis of this statement that varieties of sweets, food items etc were regularly being made on the stalls of sweet-makers then only his pan can remain burning always.

Despite the influence of Buddhism and *Vaishnavism*, non-vegetarian food items were also popular amongst masses. Besides this vegetarian foods were certainly popular and barley, wheat and rice were common food grains. There is several types of rice like shali, kalam and nivar. Because of large number of cows, milk, butter ghee and curd were available to the people. During those days, cow-worship was a part of peasant culture because bullocks used for ploughing fields and cow-milk is used for making curd, butter and ghee and other food items in various forms. In cooking food use of spices were very common. At least we can found there is a clear indication of using spices like cardamom, lavang (clove) and chilly etc. Another important item in salt of modern age was known to the people of that age also and it must have been used along with other spices in preparing food. Even in those days welcoming the guests is an inseparable part of Indian rural or peasant culture.

Despite influence of *Vaishnavism* and Buddhist religion, people of that era used the food items like meat and fish as these iterm had acquired main place. It seems that meat was obtained not only from hunted animals but also it obtained from slaughtering animals as there were slaughter houses was regularly in function where meat of pet animals were easily available. Fish was also enlisted in the diet of common masses. In this context, the statement of Fa-Hien proved that people did not domesticate pigs and chickens and they did not sale animals. There were no slaughtering shops nor there were liquor shops[36] present. Because the great traveller Fa-Hien saw the things in the perspective of the Buddhist religion. Almost towards the end of that age Huen Tsang wrote that people ate bread and rice and other grains with milk and sugar and other preparations made of these items and also they used mustard oil. Besides these, the meat of goat and sheep is also taken at that time. Some meats were also prohibited and practising of consuming liquor was a common thing.

Several types of clothes were popular among the people of that age. Besides cotton, silk and woolen clothes were also in use. Dukus, Anshuk, Uttariya, Ushmish, Stananshuk Stanapatta names indicate that during this age stitched clothes were very rarely used. One cloth was used to cover the lower portion of the body and another was used to cover the upper portion of the body. Men were found of wearing beautiful garments. They wore, white milky and colured dresses also. Amongst colours blue, red, saffron, green, kusumbhi and kumkum were in use generally by the common people.

In order to remove monotony of busy life common people used various instruments of entertainment. People of that age believed that entertainment was a means to double the capacity of life and working capacity. They used dramas, gambling, bull fight, story-telling, social function music dance as means of entertainment.

Drama houses (theatres) were born in that age. This was the age of development and climax of cultural dramas of Kalidas. There were dramas houses we got its enough evidence in literature. Dramas of that age were the best means of entertainment at the same time they reined the cultural interest in the society and also highlighted the bright side of spirituality. Enacting dramas used to be through the medium of dance playing musical instruments and singing. In social functions people participated in collectively and enjoyed it. On the occasion of any festival or function all the *varnas* and classes people participated and enjoyed equally and devotedly. Another aspect was seen on the occasion of social function whether the peole from high and low, poor and rich, educated- and uneducated, Brahmin and Shudras all were participated with full zest by shedding their emotional differences.

From the above discussions we should not understand that peasants were leading very happy and contented life during that period. Factually, the situation was just opposite. The magnitude of land donations and the rise of the middlemen led them imposition of excessive taxes which made their lives miserable. Therefore, against contemporary system, the attitude of peasants became revolting due to indifferent and inhuman approach of tax collectors and such type of inferences could be seen from the literary sources.[37] In Jataka books such rebellious attitude of the peasants is presented through Smrities, symbols and medium of stories. Peasant community secretly opposed those who captured most of their produce.

A common form of peasant's opposition can be traced when most of the unhappy lots migrated to another country.[38] If the nature of rules became exploitative and unbearable peasants left their lands and houses to run away to some other places and settled there. In such situation, when shifting was not possible though they lived there they delayed in payment of taxes or denied such payment.[39] Thus running away was a threat against revenue. Against revenue exploitation this was not only done by house-holders, rather artisans and slaves also did the same. There was mentioned of a story that a peasant disturbed by the interest on loan migrated to another land where he could live in peace.[40]

Jataka books made it clear that another method of showing discontent by the peasants was to stop roads and disturb communication.[41] Through these sources, it is clear that the payment of wages was made either in cash or in grains. In ancient India due to increase in money circulation and marketisation, it had became easier to purchase labour of a worker which resulted in fastest growth of working class system.[42] It is mentioned in a Jataka[43] that a trader fixed at 200 coins per cent for carts for five carts with a worker but on the conclusion of the work he paid 500 coins at the rate of 100 coins per cart. Therefore, as a revolt the worker kept the road blocked until he was paid the balance amount that was fixed. Peasant's anger and discontentment is also reflected in other Jatak stories 43.

Another method of the workers revolt was also the use of indecent language and foul language. This language is different from the languages of others.[44] They have their own languages and own phrases and proverbs which is to express resistance against oppressive relations of the exploiters. Due to this in a village—a ploughman and his master, an old woman, boys and all in as much as frogs even are heard cursing the king, this is mentioned.[45] A cursing word is a word born out of pain and trouble there is an example of a house-holder beating a plough man and his wife, because they were cutting fun of his voice.[46] In some Jatakas, there is also mention of wordless expressions as protest these all symbols show protest of their own condition which was prevalent at that time.

Protesting can be seen in another method in the form of thefts and robberies committed by the peasants. Evidences of these are mentioned in the Jatakas. It is described in nearly twenty-five Jatakas. During post-Vedic period, the king and some individual land-owners together took a vast population of a huge proportion within the net of their exploitation and compelled them to sell their labour for their livelihood.[47] Getting ruined thereby some people accepted theft and robbery as their profession.[48] According to Jataka, due to severe famine, the oppressed and suppressed people unable to earn their livelihood so they were resorted to theft and robbery as their main source of livelihood. Moreover, drought, famine and the escalation of high prices gave birth to such factors due to which incidents of robbery increased.[49] By the collected evidence, it is clear that mostly took shelter in jungles[50] they attacked the caravans[51] of landowners[52] and traders of the towns[53] and robbed them. It is mentioned in Jataka that rather than earning livelihood from agriculture and trade, a man gathered five hundred robbers and became their leader.[54] In another Jataka book, it has been told in 2-3 encounters with them soldier used to write a letter to the king to inform him that they are unable to suppress them.[55] The king then launched attack against them to suppress them. That proves that such type of activities like theft and robbery was organised in the form of social unrest and protest at its initial form.[56]

The boarder rebellions mentioned in the Jatakas should be seen as peasants' revolts.[57] Near twenty Jatakas mention such rebellions some of such rebellions were as a result of political enmity which were pointers to the fact that the geographical boarders of the states in those days were not settled in a proper way. In three Jatakas, it is mentioned that people running away to boarder rebutted areas for their livelihood to escape from the clutches of cruel form of revenue system,[58] famine[59] and conspiracies scripted by the king.[60] It is written in one Jataka that the fact of Bodhisatwa was burnt twice which was located on border and also they destroyed the seeds of the villagers.[61] All these make it clear that due to over exploitation of peasants such type of machinery was active. In such a situation, the only away left for the peasants was to protest against these inhuman activities of the state.[62]

References

1. Baudhayan Dharmsutra 11.36.33-34, Manusmriti, 4-213.
2. Kamasutra, 1.4.2.
3. V.K. Thakur, Urbanisation in ancient India, New Delhi 1981, page 182-92.

4. Vajasneyi Smahita.xvi.18.33, Sudhakar Chattopadhyay, the evolution of sects in ancient India, page-11.
5. Sudhakar Chattopadhyay, above referred page-11.
6. Arian, 3, 7.
7. Frazer Golden Baug volume 2, page 508.
8. Mahabharata.
9. Arthasastra,11.24.
10. Sudhakar Chattopadhyay above referred page 78.
11. Strabo, 9, 10.69.
12. Same, x, vi, 39.
13. Social Oraganisation, page 211.
14. Same IV. page 239.
15. Jatak iv 104 (cowell).
16. Raghuvansham, 9.43; 7.27.
17. Ritusanhar, 3.1.10, 16,4.1,8,18,5.1,16, Raghuvansham, 15.78,17.53.
18. Raghu, 4.37 Kumaro, 5.47.
19. Shakuo, page 94.
20. Ritu, 5.16.
21. Malo, page 42.
22. Same, page 81shaku, page 62, vikeamo, page-65.
23. Raghu, 2 .63.
24. Same, 1.45.
25. Vikaramo, page71.
26. Raghuvansih 10.51.54.
27. Kumar, 8.72.
28. Shakuo, page 55, malo, page 33-34.
29. Shakuo, page 184, 206.
30. Raghuo, 4.46.
31. Same, 47.

32. Same, 6.57.
33. Raghuo, 5.78.
34. Vikramao, page 71.
35. Malavikagnimitram, vol 2, page 289.
36. Record of Buddhist kingdom translated by James Legge, page 43.
37. Eric R. Woolf, peasants, New Jersey, 1966, page 107.
38. Irfan Habib, Ashes in Indian history towards a Marxist perception, Delhi 1997, page 110.
39. A Bose Social and Rural Economy of Northern India Calcutta 1997, page 268.
40. Jatak, V, ed. 520.
41. Same, 1, ed 125 and 127.
42. Same, iv med 406.
43. Same1, ed 156.
44. Kunch Elaith Productive labour-conciousness and history (ed) Shahid Amin and Dipesh Chakravorty Sub-altern Studies vol ix, Delhi 1997, page 165-200.
45. Jatak, v, ed 52.
46. Same 11, ed. 199.
47. R.S. Sharma: Shudraj ancient India delhi,1980 page111-112.
48. Jataka, vi, ed 547.
49. David Armod Dacoity and rural crime in madras, 1860-1940 journal of peasant studies, vo 17,no. 2 page 165.
50. Jataka, I nos 48, 59,60,76; ii no. 2, page 165.
51. Same, 1 nos 60,76,11. No. 265.
52. Same, ii, nos 267.
53. Same, iii nos 318,419.
54. Same, I nos 279.
55. Same, I no. 120.

56. E.J. Hobsbom, primitive rebels, Manchester, 1969, page, 2-96.
57. Ranjeet Gupta (ed) Sub-altern Studies vol ii, New Delhi 1982, page 43.
58. Jataka 1 no 77, iii, no 302; no, 520.
59. Same, 1 no 526.
60. Same, vi, no 539.
61. Same 1, no 130; iv, no. 429.
62. Gautam Bhadra two frontier uprising in Mughal India Ranjeet Guha (ed) Sub-altern studies, Delhi page 1983, page 59.

Conclusion

A detailed conclusion and complete discussion on the condition of peasants in India (200 - 600 AD) reveals that the condition of peasants kept on deteriorating gradually during this period. At the beginning, free-agricultural land was more and taxes were low, but in the later period because of the system of land donation there was reduction in the areas of free-agricultural land. On the other hand, donated lands were free from tax which caused a loss of state revenue. In order to compensate this loss burden of taxes on peasants went on increasing. Due to these, the economic and social conditions of the peasants were bound to fall. The later period of our study became the age of feudal lords, huge dominant religious class and big and small kings, Maharajas, rich people and traders for them this was like golden age, but so far as common masses and peasant were concerned they kept on going under the grinding wheels of exploitation all new one after the other. Particularly, because of the gradual increase in the influence of feudalism poor workers had to pass through the ordeals of labour without wage and the stage of half slaves.

Under land donation system, donees and high officials were donated land. The king absolved himself even from the responsibility of protecting his subjects and the subjects there were the vitims ofthe exploitation of land-owners and this important fact has often been shown that the victors dealt with a defeated according to their whims and fancies and imposed on them such rules as they wished and saved their own class interest and used economic interest of the defeated status. Gupta rulers were also victors in Ganga area who increased their prestige by marital relation and later on clamped this vast area and its agricultural and economic system in feudal structure.

Feudal system on land began in this period. In Central India and Bengal there are several examples of king and landlords donating lands to Brahmins and temples *Jagirdar* used to give a whole village in donation. In Bengal there used to be approval of the government officials for the purpose and also taxes were waved. But in Central India even governmental relaxations also were there. The government used to relinquish its little on every claim of revenue and used to leave the privilege of depositions. The right to rule over the inhabitants was also given to the donees, and the people were informed to pay the taxes to the donees in place of the orders, though arrangement of protecting the subjects was retained by the state. Through several land grant inscriptions, we come to know about land donations given by Gupta ruler as well.

In this period among the two most important tendencies, one was that the feudal lords or subordinate rulers of Gupta kings that donees were donated lands with revenue and administrative freedom and entire villages were donated and the second was that Gupta rulers did establish relations on the basis of unilateral agreements. Taking all things together in Gupta system of rule we find specialties of feudalism very conspicuous and visible. In fact, during the Gupta period, he rule lead the foundation of that administrative system which in later period was going to be completely feudal. This saying of Kosambi that obedience had tied peasants, slaves and dependents with feudal chiefs in chain, looks very correct.

What was the nature of land ownership in the society of Gupta period is not a matter of dispute within itself. From the sources of that time we come to know that there were three types of land ownership: personal or individual land ownership, state land ownership and collective land ownership. Ancient law books particularly by the law of the writers approve this law that the king is the protector of the land, orphan children till they grow, adult or complete their education. According to law makers in principle king had the little over the entire land due to which he realised revenue taxes from the peasants. Even if he had no title in principle over the land, he realised taxes in lieu of the protection provided to them as his wages. During the last part of this age, some particular types of statements such as land is the beloved or wife or earth is like a bride to be enjoyed by the king, this provides a glimpse of feudalism and the king seems to be so sovereign, land-owner in principle.

But now under certain conditions, certain persons were made owners of vast areas of land who could provide land or snatch away land at will. Proletarian class without taking anything did domestic works. Burden of taxes was increased on poor. Due to such donations wide power of religious institutions on economic fields got established. Along with this arrangement of individual donating lands gave birth to feudalism which continued between 500 ADto 1000 AD. Due to this, rural self-dependence increased and importance of urbanisation and guilds started declining. The system of sub-in-feudation was establishment which had most detrimental effect on the land in the form of exorbitant taxes. During Gupta period, agriculture being tied to several laws economically, through departmental arrangements, land was given a well-organised form, there are proofs available for this which have been analysed in earlier chapters.

During this period, the demand for cultivable agricultural land was too high and we get sufficient indications for that. During this period three types of land-ownership existed: king (Bhoopati), land lord (owner of the fields) and peasants (though who ploughed). This system indicates the birth of intermediary class. We get mention of the specialities of land. From this we know importance of land. Plough was among the most important agricultural implements. In Amarkosh, there are five names of plough mentioned. Brishaspati describes plough share of eight pounds and four fingers wide, which were definitely made of iron. With the help of such heavy ploughs fallow might have been ploughed deeply. Peasants careless about cultivation were punished. This is an indication of widening exploitation of the peasants by the state. Now, due to increasing burden of taxes, peasants were trying to switch over to the field of independent production more and more. Such fields being under the control of the king were the peasants doing farming and not under the control of the intermediary class. They paid taxes straight to the king. Though, whenever employees' officer of the state passed through such villages they had to do all sort of works unpaid. Land owners could extract work from peasants as well as their women folks. We get knowledge of various types of lands from Amarkosh. It seems land was categorised on the basis of quality of land. The officer maintaining these records was called "Pustpal".

During this period, forest lands and marshy lands were converted into cultivatable lands. In order to make hilly lands cultivable taxes were being increased. From the writings of Varahmihir and Kalidas, we know about the developed form of agriculture and horticulture. In order to develop agriculture, state and citizens developed sources of irrigation and used them during this period mainly wheat, barley, paddy, sugarcane, sesamum etc crops were being cultivated. Peasants had scientific knowledge of selecting appropriate lands for different crops which they used to get production of their crops.

Gradual development in agriculture practical experience and gradually developing techniques gave a definite form to agricultural implements of Gupta period. As a result, agricultural system of that age became equipped with necessary implements. Because of extensive use of iron in agricultural implements during this period there occurred several important changes in the field of agriculture. According to the situation and time many changes took place in their shape, size and types. For example, we get description of several types of ploughs. Big ploughs were called Halo. we get descriptions of even such ploughs in which more than two bullocks were yoked in. For irrigation both natural and artificial sources were used but large number of people depended on rain.

In the context of land revenue from the source of this period we know the constitution of several new administrative units, which was mostly done by state revenue administration in order to mostly realise taxes from the peasants. But these units were not popular in all parts of the country. It is often found described on stone inscription and copper plate inscriptions and copper plate inscriptions where as from the descriptions found in *Smritis,* we come to know that the system of dividing state into different parts was continuing. From the stone inscriptions of 7th and 8th century also it is supported. Two revenue officers and a commissioner related to fees etc, are also found mentioned. In this period there used to be many officers for collecting land revenue such as *diviratrati, agrabaharika, Adrangika, dhudhikaranikam, vinay Ayuptika, sarvadhyayika bhogika aparika vishayapati* etc. But it is impossible to describe accurately their duties and works. During Gupta period, the numbers of officers related to revenue administration was more compared to the officers of post-Mauryan period. This makes it clear that in this taxes and realisation was also increasingly made on forceful basis. This at places these posts had became hereditary and several works were performed by one officer. Both of these facts are the proofs of feudalisation of revenue administration.

By settling Brahmins in tribal and forest areas by donating lands, a lot of fallow lands came under cultivation and with better climatic knowledge, improved methods of agriculture became popular. The effect of feudal development was seen on new areas as well. In order to look after these, a new officer was appointed name of this post was *agraharika*.

Thus, in between fourth to sixth-seventh century A.D may be urban economic development might have hampered but the process of gradual development of rural economy continued main specialties of this period were the expansion of rural feudal economy and the development of feudal society and culture which on the strength of basic caste structure of Indian society became the cause of its growth stage after stage feudal rulers used caste tradition in their interest in such a way that the form of the Indian societies kept on becoming more and more complex *Brahmins* and *kshatriyas* i.e., ruling *purohit* classes together divided Indian society into caste and sub castes and shattered it. This had adverse impact on peasant class.

In fact the period under study is special in Indian history because it was during those centuries only that the powers in the medieval period replaced traditions and established themselves. In order to understand the situation of peasants it is necessary to observe them in combination with critical historical forces. It is said that due to decline in commerce and trade in 3rd century AD new land relations development (were born) and by the end of 6th century AD it kept on developing regularly by the same time, forces of medieval period also emerged and came to the fore in recent decades, the beginning of this critical change has been tried to be studied in the context of situational changes taking place in the central areas of Gangetic valley importance of which is intertwined with basically changing situation of the peasants. By the arrival of second century AD a high class that was controlling the factors of production grew in population, reducing fertility of the land, reduction in rain due to large scale chopping of the forest trees and vegetations, growth in the intensity of floods and other changes affected agricultural production very badly. In this context, this matter should also be remembered that for past centuries there was no further technical change could be possible to encounter new challenges that were posed. In central Gangetic valley natural wealth was harnessed uncontrolled which continued by third century such a quake came in the field which gave rise in production which put a question mark on the very existence of entire society. In the contemporary periods of epics and puranas the description of *Kaliyuga* is only the description of symptomatic expression of this social disruption.

From third century AD attempts were made to give new form to raise endangered production. Change in the form of land donation and growth in pollution was used in the outer areas of central Gangetic valley to establish agricultural occupation and was an attempt to exploit natural wear of those areas. As a result land relations changed. Whereas earlier state and peasants have direct reactions now a class of mediators were born. In distant lands where workers related to agriculture would have been less, system of bounded labour began. Along with that illegal collections also began. It deserves attention here that the number taxes increased and number of free peasants started dwindling.

By the advent of Gupta period the ancient methods of using resources with its inherent weakness and the limitations of alternative methods in their earlier stages ruined institutional base. The possibility of shrinking surplus resulted in application of force during these 40 years on the process of area and technique based expansion. In such areas of northern India where in ancient times there was lack of dense villages, now emphasis was given on agriculturisation . In these area-wise and local states were born, the base itself for which was availability of agricultural surplus.

Along with this development in the field of agriculture taking place, in order to raise production, attention was paid towards problems related to them from the middle of Gupta period, we begin getting acquainted with this tendency. In Amarkosh, and *ghatiyantra* have been mentioned. In Kadambari, Banabhatta has also described "*Jalghati yantra*". Alongwith this technique related with manuring also improved. Despite past knowledge of manures during middle part of Gupta period only a clear progress in this regard was registered. This fact is made clear by the books of this stage such as Brihatsamhita to krishi parashar, upvan vinod etc. Brihatsamhita discusses improvements in the methods of preparing seeds. Krishi Parashar also emphasises on this matter.

According to him seed should be collected during January-February, it should be dried in the sun, thereafter dust and other waste materials should be removed there after it should be used and it should be kept away grown fire, smoke and water. During this period number of annual crops also increased where as in earlier times only two crops have been discussed now three crops were grown in a year. Ritusanghar describes two separate paddy crops during *sharad* and *hemant* seasons and besides that rabi crops also. In Brihatsamhita summer winter and spring season crops have been mentioned.

Growing importance of agriculture and production relations being influenced by this has an important example-mutual equation between Brahmin class and agriculture under event fundamental changes. Legal experts of the ancient times permitted Brahmins only during emergency period but from 6th century onwards it was accepted that Brahmins should also do farming Parashar goes to the extent of saying that *panchmahayagyas* should be performed by Brahmins only with the grains produced by themselves. There is another proof also of this growing social relation agricultures code of punishment related with agricultural offences made much stiffer. From available evidence, this becomes very much clear that paradoxical to the past offenders of this category were now being given physical punishment and along with that they were placed in the category of sinners and thus arrangement was made for their punishment even after death. Every resistance and negative activity linked to agricultural economy was placed in the list of crimes.

In the emerging feudal society while on the one hand power of the state was weakening on the other hand control on agricultural system was increasing. Some scholars have considered absence of the half slaves an important element of agricultural exploitation within period this period from the absence of feudal relations. But in this effort they have denied the original form of the production relation of the contemporary India. This is also accepted fact of social history that feudal production relations which is reflected in the power equation of contemporary forces is purely decided by the physical forces or the base of masterly relation is obvious physical control over the life style of producers. In the context of this analysis the elements of slavery emerges out on the front. In fact slavery has been underlined as a related class where the situation of lab our is such that till it remains under the control of workers they themselves remain as other than workers, in this context they become a part of production for the land owners or therefore, workers became a part of property of the land owner which defines slavery. A part of his labour was usurped in the name of production tax by the master, whatever maybe the form of usurpation. During the period under discussion new developed power structure and along with this a ruling class emerging in villages, which was neutral towards central powers was always trying to establish its control over peasants, as a result of these restraints, imposed on the peasants and they became slaves of peasants in contemporary society and appears as an irrevocable fact of history.

Bibliography

(A) Original Evidence Books

(1) Inscription

Goyal, Shri Ram: Prachin Bharatiya Abhilekh Sangrah, Jaipur, 1982, Guptakalin Abhilekh, Merath.

Fleet, J.F: Corpus Inscriptionum, Indicarum Varanasi 1963 (Trans, Girija Sankar Prasad Mishra, Rajasthan Hindi Gram Academy, Jaipur).

Mirashi, V. P.: Vakatak Rajvansh Ka Itihas Tatha Inscriptions Varanashi, 1964.

Upadhyay, Vasudo: Gupta Inscriptions, Patna, 1974.

Gupt, P.L.: Prachin Bharat Ka Pramukh Abhilekh, Bhag 2, Varanasi, 1983. (2) Videshi Granth Avam Yatra – Vivaran.

Gules, H.A: The Travels of Fahien, London, 1923.

Varma, Jaganmohan (Trans.): Chini Yatri Fahian Ka Yatra vivaran New Delhi, 1996.

Leggae - Fahien, Oxford , 1886.

Bill, Samuel - Chinise Accounts of India, Calcutta 1957 – 58 Buddhist records of the Western World, London. 1884 (3) Sanskrit Books.

Amarkosh Ed., Hargovind Shastri, Varanasi, 1968.

Aryamanju Shrimodkalpah – Ed. T. Ganapati Shastri, Trivendrum 1935 A Pastamb Dharmasastra.

Gautam, Vashistha and Baudhayayan (ed): F. Maxmuler, Oxford 1889.

Vasthyankrit Kamasutra Ed. Devavrat Shastri, Varanashi, 1964.

Kalidas - Granthawali, Vaman And Jayadityakrit Ed. Sitaram Chaturvedi, Aligarh, 1950.

Kashika Vritti - Ed. Bhagwat Prasad Tripathi, Banaras, 1890.

Kamandakiya Nitisar - Ed. Vidya Sagar, J.P., Calcutta , 1875.

Katyayan Smriti – Ed. Narayan Chandra Bandyopadhyay, Calcutta, 1917.

Narad Smriti - Trans. J. Jauly, S.B.E, Khand – 33, Varanasi, 1961.

Pauranik last of the dynasties of the Kali age - F.E Pargiter, Oxford 1913.

Brihaspati Smriti Trans. J. Jouly, S.B.E, Part 33, Oxford.

Manu Smriti Ed. Pranjeewan Sharma, Bombay 1913.

Mrichahhakatikam Ed. Ramanuj Ojha, Varanasi, 1966.

Mahavastu : Paris, 1882 – 1897.

Mahavansh : Jeejar, - P.T.S, London, 1908.

Milindhanho Ed., V. Tankar, London, 1880, Trans, T.W.Rizday Vids, S. B. E., Oxford, 1890-94.

Markandey Puran Ed., K.M. Banerjee, Calcutta 1862.

Matsya Puran : S. N. Apte , Poona 1907.

Yagyavalkyasmriti, Ed. T. Ganapati Shastri (Balkrira Tika) Trivendram, 1924.

Vishnusmriti Ed. J. Jauly, Calcutta, 1881.

Vishnu Puran geetapress, gorakhapur, Trans H.S. Wilson, 5 Volumes, download 1864-70.

Varahmihirkrit Trans .Achyutanand Jha Sharma , Brihatsamhita Varanasi, 1959.

Mrichchkatikam R.D. Karmakar, Poona, 1997.

Sheekranitisar Ed. B. K. Sarkar, Allahabad 1914.

Agrawal, Jagannath Modern Books Researches in Indian Epigraphy, And Numismaties, New Delhi, 1986.

Agrawal, Vasudeosharan -Gupta Art, Banaras, 1977.

Adya . G. L. Early Indian Economics, Bombay, 1936.

Ayanger, K.B. Rangaswami -Aspects of Ancient Indian Economics.

S. Krishnaswami -Studies in Gupta History, Madras 1928.

Ambedkar, Collections of speeches and writings 1st

Dr. Babasaheb -English, Education, Department, Maharastra, Bomb ay, 1989.

Altakar A.S. State and government in Ancient India, Varanasi, 1855.

The position women in Hindu Civilization, Varanasi, 1938.

Upadhyay, Bhagwat Sharma-Kalidas ka bharat, bagh -1,2, Varanasi 1969.

Upadhyay Basudeo-gupta Samrajya Ka Itihas, Lucknow, 1969. (Bagh-1,2). Allahabad, 1939.

Cunningham, A. Hind Ancient geography of India, Varanasi, 1875.

Kane P.V. - History of Dharmasastra , Bhag 1-4, Pune, 1930-46.

Kumar, Navin - Archeological excavations in Bihar, Patna, 1999.

Kosambi, Damodar Dharmanand – The Culutre and Civilisation of Ancient India in Historical Outline, London, 1965.

An Introduction to the Study of Indian History, Bombay, 1956.

Kher N.N : Agrarian and Fiscal Economy in the Maurya and post-Maurya age, New Delhi, 1979.

Khoshala, Sarala : Gupta Civilization, New Delhi,1982.

The emperial guptas, 2 Volumes, Varanashi, 1974-1979.

Gupta, Parmashwari Lal- Gupta Samrajya, Varanashi, 1970.

The imperial guptas 2 Volumes, Varanashi, 1974-1979.

Gokhale, B.B. Samudragupta and his times in Mumbay 1962.

Gopal, Lalanji: The Ecomomic Life of Northern India, Varanashi 1965.

History of Agriculture In Ancient India,Varanashi, 1981.

Goyal, Shriram: A history of the Emperial Guptas, Allahabad 1967.

Gupta Avam Samaklin Rajvansh, Allahabad 1969.

Samudragupta Parakramank, Meerat,1987.

Gupta Samrajya Ka Ithas, Jodhpur, 1995.

Indian Art of gupta Age, from Pre-Classical Roots of The Emergence of Medieval Trends (ed,), Jodhpur, 2000.

An Introduction to Numismatics, Jodhpur,1994.

The Wonder That was Gupta India, E d; Jodhpur, 1998.

Ghoshal U.N.: A History of Indian Political Ideas, Bombay, 1959.

Hindu Revenuee System, Calcutta 1929.

Hindu Rajas Vyawastha Ka Itihas, (Trans. Ajay Mitra, Shastri, New Delhi , 1997.

The Agrarian System In Ancient India, Calcutta, 1930.

Chakaladar, H.C. Social Life in Ancient India, (Studies in the Kamsutra)

Chanana, Devraj : Slavery in Ancient India, New Delhi, 1986.

Chakravorty, H.P. : Trade and Commerce in Ancient India, Calcutta, 1966.

Chaudhary Radhkrishna – Prachin Bharat ka Arthik Itihas, Patna 1986.

Visnoi, Savita – Economic Status of Woman In Ancient India, Jodhpur, 1993.

Vishwash, T.K., Tatha Bhogendra Jha – Gupta Sculptures, Banaras, 1985.

Jayaswal, Kashi Prasad – Hindu Polity, Banglore, 1943.

Jayaswal, Gyaneshwari – Prachin Bharat Me Pashupalan, Patna, 1987.

Nar F.E: A History of Domesticated Animals, London, 1963.

Jain, Kialash Chandra – Prachin Bharat Me Samajik Avam Arthik Sansthayen, Bhopal, 1971.

Joshi, M.C: Princes and Polity In Ancient India, Merath , 1986.

Jha Dwijendra-Mauryottar Tatha Gupta Kalin Rajaswa Byawastha, Narayan New Delhi, 1977.

Ed., Bharatiya Samantawad, Rajya Samaj Aar Vichardhara, Delhi, 1999.

Thakur, Vijay Kumar – Towns in Pre- Modern India, Patna, 1993.

Historiogaphy of Indian Feudalism, Patna, 1989.

Thakur, Vijay Kumar- Ed. Peasant in Indian History,

Avam A. Anshuman - Part 1, Patna 1997.

Thakur, Vijay Kumar, - Ed. Science, Technology and Medicine.

Krishna Kumar Mandal - In Ancient India, Patna, 2000.

Dango, Shripad Amrit – India From Primitive Communism to Slavery, Mumbai, 1949.

Day, N.L. – The Geographical Dictionary of Ancient And Medival India, London, 1927.

Day, M.C – Kalidas and Vikramaditya, Caltuttta, 1928.

R.N. Dandekar – A History of the Guptas, Poona 1941.

Dutta, Bhupendranath – Dialects of Land Economics in India, Calcutta, 1952.

Das, Deepak Ranjan – The Economic History of Ancient India, Calcutta 1944.

Dwivedi, Chandralekha – Airan Ka Rajnitik Aur Sanskritik Itihas, Delhi , 1984.

Dikshitar, B.B.R. – Gupta Polity, Madras, 1952.

Niyogi, Pushpa – Contributions to the Economic History of Northeren India, Calcutta, 1962.

Prannath – A Study in the Economic Conditions of the Ancientt India, London, 1929.

Pandey, Rajwali – Vikramaditya of Ujjayini, Varanasi 1951.

N.C. Bandhyopdhyay - Economic life and progress in Ancient India, Calcutta, 1945.

Barab, M.A.: Economic life in Ancient India, Allahabad, 1906.

Banerjee, Rakhal Das- The age of Imperial Guptas, Kashi, 1933.

Banerjee P.N.: A Study of Indian Economics, London, 1940.

Basak, Radhagovind – History of North-Eastern India, Calcutta, 1934.

Buddha Prakash : Aspects of Indian History And Civilization, Agra,1965.

Basham A.L.: The Wonder that was India, London Adbhut Bharat, Agra, 1988

Block, Mark: Feudal Society, 2 Volumes, London, 1965.

Booch, M. A.: Economic life in Ancient India, Bombay, 1924.

Belin S.: Slate –and Commerce in the Romen Empire up to 300, Stock home, 1958.

Bernet, L. D.: Antiquities of India, London 1913.

Political Connection of Ancient India with the west London, 1971.

Majumder, Ramesh Chaduri : Corporate Life in Ancient India, Calcutta 1922.

Majumdar Tatta Altekar (Ed.): The Vakatak Gupta Age, Delhi, 1960.

Mazumdar Tatha Pusalkar (Ed.) : The Classical Age, Mumbai, 1962.

Mukherjee, Radhakrishna : The gupta Empire, Mumbai, 1947.

Mehta ganga Prasad: Chandragupta Vikramditya, Allahabad 1932.

Maity S.K.: The Emperial Guptas and Their Times, New Delhi, 1975.

Economic Life of Northern India in The gupta period, AD - 300-500, Calcutta, 1958.

Satish Chandra: Sarthvah, Patna, 1953.

Yadav, B. N.S.: Society and Culture in Northern India in the Twelfth Century, Allahabad, 1973.

Yadav, Achchelal : Prachin Bharat Mein Krishi, Varanasi, 1980.

Radhesharan : Samudragupta, Delhi 1969.

Roy Uday Narayan: Gupta samrat Aur Unaka kal, Allahabad, 1971 Studies in Ancient Indian History and Culture, Allahabad 1969.

Roy, Jaymal : The Rural-Urban Economy And Social Changes In Ancient India, Delhi, 1974.

Ray Chaudhary, HemChandra Political History of Ancient India, Calcutta, 1923.

Lal Angne : Sanskrit Baudhha Sahitya Me Bharatiya Jeevan, Banaras, 1974.

William Goatfeed: The Art of Gupta India, New Delhi 1883.

Sharma, Ramvilash : Indian Itihas aur Aitihasik Bhautikwad, New Delhi 1992.

Sharma, Ramsharan: Parambhik Bharat Ka Artthik Aur Samajik Itihas, Delhi 1992.

Purva Madhyakaleen Bharat Ka Samanti Samaj Aur Sanskriti, Delhi, 1996.

Bhartiya Samantwad, Delhi, Delhi, 1993.

Prachin Bharatiya Rajnitik Vichar Avam Sansthyan, Delhi 1977.

Prachin Bharat Me Bhautik Sanskriti Aur Samajik Sanrachana, Delhi Shudron ka Prachin Itihas, Delhi, 1992

Prachin Bharat me Nagaro Kapatan, New Delhi, 1995.

Shastri, Raghunandan: Gupta Vansh Ka Itihas, Lahore, 1932.

Saletore, R.N.: Life in the Gupta Age, Bombay, 1943.

Samaddhar J.N.: Economic Condition of Ancient India, Calcutta, 1922.

Singh, Prem Kumar: Prachin Bharatiya Krishi Avam Tadjanit Samasyaon Ka Adhyayan, Muzaffarpur, 1987.

Spellman, J.W.: Political Theory of Ancient India, London, 1964.

Smith, V.A.: Early History of India, Oxford, 1910.

Husain, S.A.Q. : The Economic History of India , Part - 1 Calcutta, 1962.

Hoyat, Robert S.: Feudal Institutions; causes and consequences of decentraliations (Samanti Sansthayan – Vikendrikaran Ke Karan Ya Parinam) Hott Rinehard And Winston, Newyork, 1961.

Index

B

C

H

I

J

K

M

N

T

U

V